WORK, FOR GOD'S SAKE

SARUM THEOLOGICAL LECTURES

WORK, FOR GOD'S SAKE

Christian Ethics in the Workplace

Esther D. Reed

DARTON·LONGMAN+TODD

First published in 2010 by
Darton, Longman and Todd Ltd
1 Spencer Court
140 – 142 Wandsworth High Street
London SW18 4JJ

ISBN 978-0-232-52761-2

A catalogue records for this book is available from the British Library.

Phototypeset by Kerrypress Ltd, Luton, Bedfordshire.
Printed and bound in Great Britain by Thomson Litho, East Kilbride, Scotland

CONTENTS

PREFACE

Sarum College mounts, in collaboration with the Dean and Chapter of Salisbury Cathedral, an annual series of public lectures, which aim to move from year to year through a range of different areas of pressing theological concern, and to make available the highest quality of research in an attractive and readily accessible form. The lectures are subsequently published by Darton, Longman and Todd.

The first such series (1999) was Professor Mary Grey's *The Outrageous Pursuit of Hope*, followed by Professor David Catchpole's *Resurrection People* (2000). Then came Professor Grace Davie on *Europe: The Exceptional Case* (2001); and Professor Brian Thorne on *Infinitely Beloved: The Challenge of Divine Intimacy* (2002). Archbishop Rowan Williams opened up *The Quest of the Historical Church: Why Study Church History?* (2003), and was followed by Professor Frances Young on *Towards a Biblical Spirituality* (2004), Canon Vernon White on *Life after Death* (2005), and Professor Richard Bauckham on *Beyond Stewardship: The Bible and the Community of Creation* (2006).

This book has grown from the Sarum Lectures delivered by Esther D. Reed in the spring of 2007. She is extremely grateful to Sarum College, and the Dean and Chapter of Salisbury Cathedral, for the invitation to deliver the lectures.

She wishes especially to thank David Catchpole for his assistance, all those who shared experiences and insights which contributed to her preparation, and to acknowledge with gratitude the particular insights of Keith Ellis.

ACKNOWLEDGEMENTS AND ABBREVIATIONS

Unless otherwise stated, Scripture quotations in this publication are from the New Revised Standard Version. The following abbreviations indicate the alternative versions that are used occasionally:

NKJV New King James Version
NASB New American Standard Bible
NIV New International Version
JSB *The Jewish Study Bible*, ed. A. Berlin and M. V. Brettler (New York: OUP Inc., 2004); the TANAKH translation is copyright © 1985, 1999 the Jewish Publication Society).

St Nicholas (Russian) [IP-M527] printed with the kind permission of St Vladimir's Seminary Press, www.svspress.com.
Resurrection of Christ [IP-L927] printed with the kind permission of St Vladimir's Seminary Press, www.svspress.com.

Chapter 1

THANK GOD IT'S FRIDAY?

'I do not like work even when someone else does it,' Mark Twain is reputed to have remarked. He was commenting on the prospect of a sailor rowing him twenty-eight miles to Marseilles from where a silhouetted mountain range was said to resemble the reclining figure of 'the great commander' Napoleon.[1] The association of work with toil, effort and discomfort offended Mark Twain's gentle sensibilities and he wrinkled his nose at the mere idea. It wasn't even he who was to do the rowing!

In the more famous *Adventures of Tom Sawyer*, Mark Twain observed: 'Work consists of whatever a body is obliged to do. Play consists of whatever a body is not obliged to do.'[2] Work is not something one would choose to do – at least while fishing, lounging on the front porch and telling stories remained options. In some similarity, Oscar Wilde, the Irish dramatist and social commentator of the nineteenth century, commented that hard work 'is the refuge of people who have nothing better to do' – the implication being that one should avoid it if one can.[3]

More recently, the Dogbert character in Adam Scott's cartoon strip *Dilbert* exclaims: 'Work is for losers.' Only 'losers' submit to this degradation. 'A winner says "That's on my list [of things to do]" and never commits to a deadline.'[4] Why live holed up in your cubicle at the office? 'Build a better life by stealing office supplies,' writes the master of office angst.

Most of us need to work for our living, however. For better or worse, either as employees or as self-employed, many of us spend much of our lives in paid work. Work – in this everyday sense – is that part of the day devoted to economic ends. Its instrumental value allows us to pay the bills and keep a roof over our heads. But what is spiritual meaning of work in our lives?

In this book, I want to shed light upon the meaning and place of work within Christian theological and ethical tradition. Our treatment of the subject is far from comprehensive. Yet it leads me to make three claims:

- in order to understand the meaning of work, one must first understand the meaning of rest;
- the predominant framework for describing a Christian ethic of work, for our purposes at least, is the resurrection of Christ Jesus from the dead. What we say about work will depend upon what we say about resurrection;
- reflection on the resurrection can orient (or reorient) the working lives of Christians in important ways.

WHAT IS WORK?

First, however, we must clarify our use of the term 'work'. Work may be conceived variously as the following, and more:

- activity or effort expended towards an end;
- paid employment or self-employment;
- a form of political oppression to be superseded;
- unpaid occupational role or voluntary activity;
- what, according to personal preferences, is irksome and restraining yet necessary;
- vocation or call;
- worship;
- saying 'yes' to life.

Work as activity or effort expended towards an end

This quasi-technical sense in which 'work' may be defined as activity or effort expended towards an end is the closest we get to a neutral definition – in the sense of its being indifferent in relation to one's own self and place in society. For instance, the term 'work' is understood in physics or chemistry to mean the product of the force used to move an object. Work is 'the amount of energy transferred to or from a body or system as a result of forces acting upon it' thereby causing its displacement.[5] It is a useful definition but not adequate for a more thoroughly theological engagement with our topic.

Work as paid employment or self-employment

More commonly, in present-day social contexts, work is understood as paid employment – a trade, profession, or other means of livelihood that provides the essentials for living. Alain de Botton's book *The Pleasures and Sorrows of Work* studies ten types of work in this sense (cargo shipping; biscuit manufacturing; career counselling; accountancy; rocket science; painting; transmission engineering; entrepreneurship; and various careers within aviation).

We might also list teaching, catering, brick-laying, journalism, policing, fire-fighting, banking, sales, lorry driving, intelligence analysing, photography, cartography, aerospace systems organisation, music, physical training, chaplaincy, dentistry, environmental health, biomedical science, and much more. These are all types of paid employment or self-employment that, for present purposes, we call *work as paid employment*. This is work tied, typically, to economic necessity in a wage-based society.

Work as a form of political oppression to be superseded

This seemingly straightforward definition, that is, work as paid employment, is not neutral or value-free, however. 'Why', asks the left-wing theorist André Gorz, 'do we say that a woman "works" when she takes care of children in a nursery school and "does not work" when she stays at home to take care of her own children?'[6] To confine the meaning of work to paid employment is to reflect a society in which paid employment occupies a central place in our collective minds, thoughts and imaginations, and where free-market capitalism ties social worth to the obtaining of a sufficient, regular income from paid work.

Only the dissidents in capitalist societies, writes Gorz, refuse to contribute to the wage-based society and decline the rights, benefits and identity conferred by social and economic citizenship. 'The essential point', he writes, 'is that "work" performs a *socially identified and normalized function in the production and reproduction of the social whole*.'[7] In other words, perceptions of social worth attach to work. An individual's social standing or sense of respect in the community is tied closely to how they make a living. Unpaid occupational roles and/or voluntary work often make non-obvious contributions to the economy and perform less socially identifiable functions than paid employment. Such roles are not in the public sphere, at least not as obviously. Hence they do not meet socially coded norms of usefulness and worth.

Gorz's challenge is that *work as paid employment* slips rapidly into work as the measurable, quantifiable labour, detachable from the worker who provides it. Echoes of Karl Marx's historical materialism and the alienation of workers from what they produce may be heard in his writings. Before dismissing his ideas too quickly, however, it is worth noting his challenge to think about work without primary reference to paid employment. Socially radical thinkers such as Jeremy Rifkin and André Gorz urge that '[w]e must dare to prepare ourselves for the Exodus from "work-based society".'[8] Their vision is for a society in which we strive to minimise paid employment – partly in response to technological advancement and the ecological crisis but also because they believe it important to human well-being to increase the amount of time spent on autonomous, self-determined activity.

Work as unpaid occupational role or voluntary activity

Work as paid employment will remain one of our primary definitions. This said, there are points at which we might agree with Rifkin and Gorz – even if our political philosophy and reasoning is different. Like Rifkin and Gorz, a Christian ethic of work will not be satisfied with thinking about work only, or even primarily, as paid employment. It is vitally important to recognise the narrowness and ideological entanglement of the meaning of the word 'work' when used in this superficially neutral sense. Furthermore, unpaid occupational roles and/or voluntary work are often neglected in studies about work. This reflects the restrictedness of dominant Western conceptions of work as tied to economic necessities and the wage-based society.

My mother worked for many years – raising children, doing jobs around the farm, caring for sick and elderly people, taking 'bed and breakfast' guests, doing endless voluntary work for church organisations, and much more. She made relatively few National Insurance contributions. Is my paid work with students more socially valuable than her many years as an unpaid youth worker? Was her vocation any less meaningful? Of course not! So it is important to be clear that our theological consideration of work includes both paid and unpaid employment. While I am concerned especially at the lack of theological engagement with formal paid employment where many church members spend two-thirds of their waking time, I hope also to give due recognition to unpaid occupational roles and/or voluntary work that are often neglected in studies about work.

Work as what, according to personal preferences, is irksome and restraining yet necessary

All this accepted, definitions of work cannot be kept entirely separate from personal preference and societal prejudice. Christian ethicist Gilbert Meilander recounts the story of the three workers breaking rocks into pieces. 'Asked what they were doing, the first answered, "Making little rocks out of big ones." The second replied, "Making a living." And the third said, "Building a cathedral."'[9] One man's drudgery is another's amusement. One woman's pleasure is another's pain. The meaning of work as it plays out in our lives has no single import or significance.

Whether a person experiences work as blessing or curse depends upon both subjective and objective factors. Personal satisfaction, or lack of it, and whether one feels a sense of vocation, are hugely significant factors alongside labour standards that provide protection for workers, among other benefits. The two are often interlinked. Personal satisfaction in the workplace is likely to be higher, we might suppose, if, for example, a floor of decent employment rights is in place, if a person receives a living wage, and if legal measures are available to prevent monopolies and destructive competition that undercut prices by compromising the well-being of workers. Both sets of factors have direct bearing on the quality of personal and family life, community relations, and whether the politics of work is oriented towards common good.

Nor are subjective factors exclusively personal. Sometimes a person's social and cultural context can affect their perception of which jobs are desirable and which likely to attract opprobrium. A person's social and cultural context can affect their perception of what counts as 'work' and what counts as 'leisure'. When my husband refers in jest to mowing the lawn as one of the many 'labours of Chuck', alluding to the endless and never-completed work of Sisyphus in Greek mythology, condemned to roll a boulder uphill only to watch it roll back down, I know only too clearly that he'd rather be doing something other than pushing the lawnmower up and down that Saturday afternoon. Use of the phrase 'labours of Chuck' associates an essentially leisure activity with the necessities of the workplace.

The philosopher and classicist J. P. Toner defines work and leisure in terms of symbols and how they function for us both personally and communally. For the wife who enjoys looking at a freshly mown lawn, the lawnmower is associated with relaxation and weekend leisure time. For Chuck, the husband, the symbol of the lawnmower is ambiguous. Chuck associates the lawnmower with work. To borrow Toner's words, the lawnmower is part of 'a system of symbols which acts to establish a feeling of restraint and effort by formulating a sense of obligation and necessity'.[10] Mowing the lawn contrasts with leisure, which he understands as a system of symbols characterised by 'a feeling of freedom and pleasure by formulating a sense of choice and desire'.[11]

Despite representing a weekend activity undertaken in those few hours of the week not spent for his employer, the lawnmower represents necessity and lack of freedom. Chuck's social and cultural context demands that he mow the lawn throughout the summer months. Failure to do so would impact negatively upon the neighbourhood. This, in turn, has a bearing upon his perception of a routine leisure-time activity. The unspoken pressures of his social and cultural context turn this simple activity into an unwelcome chore.

Work as vocation or call

A question that arises especially, although not exclusively, for Christian people when defining 'work' is whether to use the word 'vocation'. Should every Christian answer: 'My vocation!' to the question: 'What is work?' or 'What is work *to you*?' So, for instance, Martin Luther taught that *all* Christians, not just monks, had a vocation, and that every type of work performed by a Christian can be a vocation.[12] John Calvin wrote movingly of God's fatherly care toward every person in their daily labours:

> the Lord bids each one of us in all life's actions to look to his calling … The magistrate will discharge his functions more willingly; the head of the household will confine himself to his duty; each man will bear and swallow the discomforts, vexations, weariness, and anxieties in his way of life, when he has been persuaded that the burden was laid upon him by God.[13]

These great reformers of the Church developed strong theologies of vocation, that is, the calling to which God has appended one's name.

Yet we must be careful when handling this notion that work is a vocation, call, or that which God has given us to do. When combined in later Calvinism with the idea of election, the idea developed that God has appointed every person to their station in life and that their duty is to serve God willingly in this station – regardless of meniality or exploitation – to the best of their ability. Sometimes referred to as the 'Protestant work ethic' of the industrial era, the idea that work is a God-given vocation, and therefore a noble and ennobling activity, meshed with the needs of industrialists for workers who would tolerate appalling factory conditions.

The Church's record in this respect has been criticised by high-profile scholars including the social critic Zygmunt Bauman. He claims that thousands of England's poor were sent as low-paid workers to the mills under the sacralising notion of vocation. Reformation theologies of vocation allowed church members to intertwine the idea of work as a vocation with the needs of burgeoning industry during the early industrial era, and to turn a blind eye to exploitation.[14] Consider George Herbert's poem 'The Elixir', which congregations often sing as a hymn:

Teach me, my God and King,
In all things thee to see,
And what I do in anything,
To do it as for thee.
A servant with this clause
Makes drudgery divine:
Who sweeps a room, as for thy laws
Makes that and th' action fine.[15]

If we accept too readily that drudgery can be made 'divine' by describing it as vocational, then important issues of human dignity, self-esteem and social justice have probably been overlooked.

Fine-sounding accounts of work as vocation are next to worthless if blind to the hellishness of lived realities. Indeed, the noted Croatian theologian Miroslav Volf has recently rejected the language of vocation for fear that it attributes spiritual honour to work that is underpaid, degrading, unsafe and exploitative, and is insensitive to lived experience. Theology today must 'lift the dead hand of "vocation" from the Christian idea of work', he writes, because of too many unfortunate associations.[16]

Most hymnals now omit the following verse from Cecil F. Alexander's hymn 'All things bright and beautiful':

The rich man in his castle,
The poor man at his gate,
He made then, high or lowly,
And ordered their estate.

Alexander's theology of vocation as expressed in this verse equates with an acceptance of the status quo. Volf rejects the language of vocation for precisely these reasons, and we must surely heed his reasons for caution. Christian talk about vocation cannot be revived unless and until fundamental issues of social justice are central to the endeavour.

There is no future for a theology of vocation, nor should there be, unless objective factors affecting the workplace (e.g. macro-economic policies aimed at full employment and legal measures to prevent monopolies and destructive competition that undercuts prices by compromising the well-being of workers) are understood to have a direct bearing upon important subjective factors (not least a sense of vocation and degree of personal preference in one's choice of job). There is no need to throw the proverbial baby out with the bath water, however. We return to this question of vocation in Chapter 3 where special study is made of St Paul's understanding of his personal vocation in relation to the broader vocation of the Church.

Work as worship

There is, of course, a sense in which work must be understood as the trade, profession, or other means of livelihood that provides the essentials for living; a Christian ethic of work cannot be understood apart from employer–employee relationship, business enterprise, the institutions of the labour market, trade unions, employers' associations and economic relations that in some way involve 'the exchange of personal service or services for remuneration.'[17] What we regard as work is affected by personal preference and societal norms, among other things. At a more basic level of human existence, however, work is a spiritual reality. One of the challenges of this book is to think about work in explicitly theological and spiritual terms. This includes the interaction between work and worship, worship and work.

'Worship is the basic activity and lifeblood of the Church.'[18] This has been true since the earliest days of Christianity when the disciples spent much time in the temple and at home praising God, breaking bread and eating together (Acts 2:46–7). The writer to the Ephesians speaks of the Christian calling to 'live for the praise of his [God's] glory' (Ephesians 1:12). In the New Testament we read of churches in Antioch and Lystra, Macedonia and Corinth worshipping God. The Book of the Revelation to John contains a vision of cosmic worship when every living creature gives glory and honour to the Father and the elders cast their crowns before his throne singing: 'You are worthy, our Lord and God, to receive glory and honour and power, for you created all things, and by your will they existed and were created' (Revelation 4:11). Of interest to us, however, is not only the work of worship but relationships between the work of worship and everyday paid employment, voluntary work, unpaid labour, and the like.

The word 'liturgy' derives etymologically from the Late Latin *liturgia* which comes, in turn, from the Greek *leitourgia* meaning public service (from Greek *laos* – people + *ergon* – work). In ancient Greek society, *leitourgia* could mean public service of any kind, for example the provision of a warship for the state or supervision of the gymnasium. In the Septuagint (a Greek version of the Jewish Scriptures redacted in the third and second centuries BC by Jewish scholars and adopted by Greek-speaking Christians) *leitourgia* is used for the public service of the temple and especially the ritual functions of the priests (e.g. Joel 1:9; 2:17.). In Luke 1:23, we read that Zechariah goes home when 'the days of his liturgy' (*hai hēmerai tēs leitourgias autou*) are over. In Hebrews 8:6, the high priest of the New Law 'has obtained a more excellent liturgy', that is, a better kind of public religious service, than that of the Temple.

The work of worship (including but not confined to the formal or informal liturgies of corporate worship) is where Christian people may best become sensitised to how the work that they do day by day finds its proper destiny in God's drama of redemption. Worship is not only where Christian people learn to interpret Holy Scripture, pray and find strength for the week, but where they may best learn an ethic of work. Worship is more than a once-a-week activity: it is a way of being or 'life orientation' for the Church and its members.[19] Worship shapes and gives content to the *ethos* (character, distinguishing marks, moral nature) of the Christian Church; it is where believers are invited especially to meet with the risen Christ. Chapter 4 thus thinks in more detail about connections between the various moments of the liturgy (we look especially at the gathering, anaphora, anamnesis, epiclesis, communion, dismissal) and the day-to-day world of work. Chapter 5 addresses how the truth of the resurrection confessed in worship is a dynamic for the practice of justice, respect, honour and good order not only within the Church but in the wider political arena.

WORK IS A SPIRITUAL TOPIC

The challenge of this book is to think about work in explicitly theological and spiritual terms. This might be to state the obvious. Yet perhaps we need to do precisely this. Lamentably, the Church in Western societies is slow to equip its people for Christian witness in their working lives and support them when the going gets tough. The evangelist Mark Greene's pamphlet *Supporting Christians at Work (without Going Insane)* confronts us with some immediate pastoral implications. Citing a member of a local congregation, he writes:

> 'I spend an hour a week teaching Sunday school and they haul me up to the front of the church to pray for me. The rest of the week I'm a full-time teacher and the church has never prayed for me. That says it all.'[20]

Britain's workplaces are filled with all kinds of people, with all kinds of problems, he writes. Illness, fear of redundancy, adultery, grief, confusion, purposelessness, promiscuity, ethical conundrums, criminal negligence, racism, dirty tricks, and so on, are common alongside more positive and welcome experiences. In such contexts, the only way of thinking available to Christian people should not be merely to start emailing colleagues with evangelistic messages or leaving adverts for the Alpha Course by the vending machine. There are times and places for evangelism.

Yet explicit witness to Christ is not the only answer to our question: 'What is God doing at work?'

The conviction that work is an explicitly theological and spiritual matter arises directly from biblical witness. Adam was placed in the garden 'to work it and take care of it' (Genesis 2:15 NIV). This is what he has been made to do and given to do. This enjoyable and rewarding work is what God requires of him in the newly created world. The Hebrew words for 'to work it and take care of it' are *'abad* and *shamar* respectively. The former implies hard work and considerable effort; *'abad* can mean forced labour. Elsewhere in the Old Testament, *'abad* carries connotations of routine work or service (Leviticus 23:7, 25 – 'do no regular work' NIV; Numbers 4:47; Nehemiah 3:5 – the work of repairing the walls of the temple). It was used especially of the work of the priests and levites in offering daily sacrifices to God (Numbers 3:7–8), as well as of servile work in bondage or slavery (Leviticus 25:39; Ezra 9:8). The *'abad* or work of the Tabernacle is its service to God (Numbers 8:26, 18:5–6).

The King James Version translates Genesis 2:15 as: 'And the Lord God took the man and put him into the garden of Eden, to dress it and to keep it.' The Hebrew *shamar* can mean to keep, tend, guard, protect, or retain. Elsewhere in the Old Testament, *shamar* implies priestly duties concerning the worshipping life of the people of Israel. We shall return to this association of work with worship. The verb is used frequently of guarding the holiness of God's sanctuary – especially in the sense of guarding against profanation by unauthorised 'strangers' (e.g. Numbers 1:53, 3:8, 10, 32, 8:26, 18:3ff., 31:30, 47; 1 Samuel 7:1; 2 Kings 12:9; 1 Chronicles 23:32; 2 Chronicles 34:9; Ezekiel 44:15f., 48:11).[21] Again, the association with worship of God is strong. When viewed canonically, that is, with reference to the theological shape of the Bible as we now encounter it given the ordering of its books, work features from the outset and is rarely distant in its meaning from some kind of association with worship.

One further point about work as a properly theological topic may be mentioned. This is that God himself works. In Exodus

20:9, God commands his people to work (*melakah*) for six of the seven days of the week. *Melakah* means occupation, business or skilled work. It is *melakah* that is forbidden on the Sabbath (Exodus 31:14–15, 35:2). Significantly, however, *melakah* is used in Genesis 2:2–3 of the work that God himself had been doing, and with which he was pleased. God himself 'rested from all the work that he had done in creation'. The Hebrew words are *bara'* (created) and *'asah* (made). Both words are used in verb forms. Of themselves, they permit us to say that God himself has been shaping, fashioning, forming, creating something new, preparing, producing, bringing things about. In the New Testament also, Jesus is recorded as saying: 'My Father is still working, and I also am working' (Greek *ergazetai/ergazomai*) John 5:17). The gods of Greek mythology were not thought of as working in the way that God the Father works. Jesus also appears to describe the entirety of his ministry as work. Both God the Father and God the Son are said to be working as they bring salvation and blessing to humankind.

Ergazomai is the standard Greek verb for labouring, earning a living, performing a task, causing something to exist. It is used numerous times in the New Testament for various types of employment with which people were occupied. The author of the Letter to the Philippians refers to the salvation of the saints at Philippi as the *ergon* that God will bring to completion at the day of Jesus Christ (Philippians 1:6) and Paul's missionary labours are described as *ergon* (Acts 13:2, 15:38). The conduct that springs from faith is referred to as *ergon* (1 Thessalonians 1:3), as are the kind of noble actions that harmonise with the good of society (Romans 13:3; Titus 3:1). *Ergon* is frequently associated with toil, struggle and hindrances (e.g. Hebrews 4:10) and used of the actions of the devil (John 8:41). Biblical authors use the same word of God's work as of human work. The daily occupation of slaves is *ergon* (Mark 13:34). The heavens and the earth are the works (*erga*) of God's hands (Hebrews 1:10). A life dedicated to the ways of God is work (*ergon*) that God will receive (Matthew 26:10; Mark 14:6; John 3:21; Acts 9:36).

The work undertaken by God's people is *God's* work: 'The Holy Spirit said, "Set apart for me Barnabas and Saul for the work (*ergon*) to which I have called them"' (Acts 13:2). As Jesus' food was 'to do the will of him who sent me and to complete his work' (John 4:34), so Jesus' disciples are also to be steadfast in their efforts, 'always excelling in the work of the Lord' (1 Corinthians 15:58).

Work as saying 'yes' to life

Yet more broadly, we affirm with Karl Barth – one of the most noteworthy Protestant theologians of the twentieth century – that *to work is to assent to the creative word of God and the very fact of our existence*. Work, says Barth, is a person's 'active affirmation of his existence as a human creature'.[22] Work, like love, is a way of saying 'yes' to life.

This definition of work is the last in our provisional list; it is also the broadest. Barth alludes not merely to a chosen profession, preferred activity or necessary means by which to make a living. Rather, he speaks of work as a mode of life. Our human nature knows, he seems to imply, that the fullness of life requires engagement in some kind of work. He does not mean that a person is fulfilled by working 9 to 5 and all this entails. His meaning is broader. He speaks of a mode of self-offering whereby our very being accords the world meaning by our welcoming the work of the day.

Barth alludes in this particular definition to work as something like the acceptance of life in the hearts of Adam and Eve before paradise was lost. We cannot, of course, regain the pre-fall state. Yet, what the Orthodox theologian Christos Yannaras calls 'life's energy' can embody in each of us a yearning for life that gets us out of bed in the morning – even if metaphorically speaking. Whether we can or cannot get out of bed physically, the work of life entails reciprocity of relation with fellow creatures. In Barth's sense of saying 'yes' to life, work entails both the receiving and giving of care, and, sometimes perhaps, the struggle to be grateful for life itself.

Chapter 2

HOLY SATURDAY AND THE CURSE OF WORK TODAY

Oscar Wilde decried work as 'the curse of the drinking classes'.[1] The biblical sense of work as curse is far more far-reaching:

> Cursed is the ground because of you;
>   in toil you shall eat of it all the days of your life;
> thorns and thistles it shall bring forth for you; …
> By the sweat of your face
>   you shall eat bread … (Genesis 3:17–19)

Despite the fact that we now live after Christ (*post Christum*) when sin is a defeated reality, both intentional and unintentional embroilment in sin seems inescapable. '[W]e are dealing not merely with any *corruptio*,' writes Karl Barth, 'but with the *corruptio optimi* … the selling and enslavement of the good man and his nature and all the actions of his nature to the service of evil and the work of his own pride.'[2] 'The wages of the labourers … [still] cry out' (James 5:4). Near-starvation wages in many so-called developing countries, consumer goods with built-in obsolescence, and environmental damage, are among the wrongs that call down divine judgement upon us.

> Hear this, you that trample on the needy,
> and bring to ruin the poor of the land, …
> buying the poor for silver
>   and the needy for a pair of sandals,
> and selling the sweepings of the wheat.
> The LORD has sworn by the pride of Jacob:
> Surely I will never forget any of their deeds.

Shall not the land tremble on this account,
and everyone mourn who lives in it ...?

So thunders the prophet Amos down the ages (Amos 8:4–6). 'The land will vomit you out for defiling it' (Leviticus 18:28), cries the Lord our God in a passage that might be read afresh today in light of the environmental crisis. The language of being held to account, subject to divine judgement and curse is not popular these days. Yet resurrection presupposes the judgement of crucifixion. God is holy. The divine 'No' to sin persists. Like John the Baptist, the Church still points away from itself to Christ and prepares the way for him by calling sinners to repentance.

John Milton, one of the finest poets of the English language, recounts the teaching of Genesis 3:16–19 in Book 9 of *Paradise Lost* as follows:

. . . And to the Woman thus his Sentence turn'd.
Thy sorrow I will greatly multiplie
By thy Conception; Children thou shalt bring
In sorrow forth, and to thy Husbands will
Thine shall submit, hee over thee shall rule.

On ADAM last thus judgement he pronounc'd.
Because thou hast heark'nd to the voice of thy Wife,
And eaten of the Tree concerning which
I charg'd thee, saying: Thou shalt not eate thereof,
Curs'd is the ground for thy sake, thou in sorrow
Shalt eate thereof all the days of thy Life;
Thornes also and Thistles it shall bring thee forth
Unbid, and thou shalt eate th' Herb of th' Field,
In the sweat of thy Face shalt thou eate Bread,
Till thou return unto the ground, for thou
Out of the ground wast taken, know thy Birth,
For dust thou art, and shalt to dust returne.[3]

The peculiar sorrows of women are multiplied greatly in the labour of childbirth and strivings with their menfolk. The judgement on Adam is no less harsh as Milton calls attention to the extension of the curse to posterity; a 'propagated curse' that will reproduce itself in subsequent generations:

> But say
> That Death be not one stroak, as I suppos'd,
> Bereaving sense, but endless miserie
> From this day onward, which I feel begun
> Both in me, and without me, and so last
> To perpetuitie; Ay me, that fear
> Comes thundring back with dreadful revolution
> On my defensless head; both Death and I
> Am found Eternal, and incorporate both,
> Nor I on my part single, in mee all
> Posteritie stands curst: Fair Patrimonie
> That I must leave ye, Sons; O were I able
> To waste it all my self, and leave ye none! (Bk 9)

Humankind would have been happier, Milton says, if

> ... it suffic'd him to have known
> Good by it self, and Evil not at all. (Bk 10)

– that is, if Adam and Eve's taste for knowledge had not tempted them to become like God.

However we interpret the sad business with the apple in biblical accounts of the garden of Eden, the association of work as curse with pain in childbirth, toil, sweat, thorns, thistles and sorrow, is clear. God's judgement is upon sin, and this has consequences for how people experience work. The accursed nature of the earth as a result of human sin defines the human condition. It profoundly affects the way we live, and especially how we either experience work or are forced to work.

THE ACCURSED NATURE OF WORK TODAY

In March 2007, we commemorated the 200th anniversary of the parliamentary bid to abolish the slave trade in the British colonies. We looked backwards to when, as the Archbishop of Canterbury reminded us, even the Church of England and its bishops owned slaves in Caribbean plantations and lived for some time off 'the historical legacy of slavery'.[4] We also looked around to the fact that slavery continues today.[5]

A Sudanese young man named Francis Bok testified before the US Senate Committee on Foreign Relations that he was captured at the age of seven from his village in Southern Sudan, and worked as a slave for ten years, before finally escaping. Investigative journalists report innumerable horrific instances of human trafficking for all forms of forced labour, including agriculture, domestic service, construction work, and sweatshops, as well as trafficking for commercial sexual exploitation.[6]

Consider the child's face on p.18. This image is from a Child Labour petition organised by the International Confederation of Free Trade Unions (ICFTU) in support of international labour standards. Would you sign the petition? At the time of writing, the petition was available at <http://www.icftu.org> and visitors to the site were invited to sign up.

The petition called on all governments to say YES to education for all children and NO to child labour, by ratifying and implementing International Labor Organisation (ILO) Child Labour Conventions 138 and 182.[7] ILO convention 138 incorporates the Minimum Age Convention 1973, which specifies that full-time workers shall not be less than 15 years. National laws may permit the employment of persons 13 to 15 years of age on light work which is (a) not likely to be harmful to their health or development, or (b) not such as to prejudice their attendance at school. Convention 182 incorporates the Worst Forms of Child Labour Convention 1999. It prohibits child slavery (including the sale and trafficking of children, debt bondage, and forced recruitment for armed conflict), child prostitution and pornography, the use of children for illicit activities (such as drug trafficking), and any hazardous work which is likely to harm the health, safety or morals of children.

The petition calls on employers to stop hiring children and urges that those children who are working should be taken out of work, rehabilitated and brought into school. Employers, governments and international institutions are called upon to provide decent jobs for adults and respect the right of workers to organise. It also calls upon global institutions such as the International Monetary Fund, the World Bank and the World Trade Organisation to respect core labour standards and make sure that programmes ensure access to free, basic education, rather than causing governments to slash education budgets.

Should we sign the petition? The ICFTU claims that respect for core labour standards is integral to building democracy, fighting poverty and development. It wants the IMF, World Bank, WTO and others to link protection of labour standards to trade deals, and declares support from trade unions in developing countries, and claims that ILO standards avoid exploitation of workers, avoid a 'race to the bottom' as countries try to undercut each other, and help eradicate poverty worldwide. Should we sign? ILO standards are international measures to enforce compliance with labour standards in developing countries. The arguments for signing seem overwhelming.

Initially surprising, therefore, is the warning sounded by organisations such as Third World Network, an Indian-based think tank devoted to development issues, and CentreSouth.[8] Both take issue with any linking of labour standards to aid or trade agreements, arguing that trade and social arrangements should be kept separate. Compulsory labour standards, they argue, quickly become protectionist and not altruistic measures. Even if such measures are intended to establish a global 'social floor', the potential damage to developing economies is great. It is better for higher labour standards to be achieved in developing countries via evolutionary methods, and this cannot be done at a speed required by external bodies. According to these organisations, international measures to enforce compliance with labour standards in developing countries (by means of sanctions or other punitive measures) as part of efforts to establish a global 'social floor' are neither desirable nor feasible.

How is judgement possible amidst such complexity? To what extent is it possible to reach the kind of judgement that might discriminate between right and wrong, and effect changes for the better? Debate surrounding the ILO campaign against child labour cited above illustrates how difficult the kind of judgement that can discriminate in such situations is likely to be. The curse of work may be broken in Christ but its effects remain evident.

As I write, the global trade union movement is holding a World Day for Decent Work (WDDW).[9] Decent Work was introduced in 1999 as a campaigning concept and agenda by the ILO with a working definition of Decent Work as follows:

> Decent work has been defined by the ILO and endorsed by the international community as being productive work for

> women and men in conditions of freedom, equity, security and human dignity. Decent work involves opportunities for work that is productive and delivers a fair income; provides security in the workplace and social protection for workers and their families; offers better prospects for personal development and encourages social integration; gives people the freedom to express their concerns, to organize and to participate in decisions that affect their lives; and guarantees equal opportunities and equal treatment for all.[10]

Global poverty campaigns will fail, its organisers say, without Decent Work. Hence 165 million trade unionists around the world are calling for work to be put centre stage in campaigns against poverty. The programme for the day includes sessions on the campaign against poor working standards in the gold industry, the rate of progress in achieving the Millennium Goals as they bear upon corporate social responsibility policies, how to improve the living standards of workers and farmers in developing countries through the better purchasing practices of businesses in the UK, why so many children in poverty in the UK come from families where at least one parent is earning, and more.

I signed the ICFTU petition – on the grounds that education is a fundamental human right set forth in the United Nations Declaration of Human Rights and, more importantly from a faith perspective, because a child would be wronged if deprived of the good of education. A young person should never be treated as if they have less worth than they do as a child of God. Wages should be high enough for parents to be able to support their children and send them to school rather than the local factory. We return in Chapter 4 to questions about 'the right to work' and the meaning of this right in diverse socio-economic contexts. For the moment, we cannot but recognise that the accursed nature of work in our world is interconnected in multiply complex ways with oppression and death, especially for the poor.

Nor is everything rosy with respect to work for the relatively well paid. In 'burnout Britain' many of us leave work exhausted at the end of every day uttering expletives under our breath at employers who seem now to require not only a fair day's work for the remuneration offered but our hearts and souls too.[11] In 2005 Madeleine Bunting's study of overwork and despair in British workplaces today, *Willing Slaves: How the Overwork Culture is Ruling our Lives*, shocked readers as she analysed the impact on individuals and families of employers 'wanting blood', that is, demanding so much that home life is damaged, workplaces have rising incidence of depression, and the threat of redundancy is commonplace.

More recently, the Trades Union Congress (TUC) has spoken of 'lip service' paid to work–life balance.[12] The Work Foundation says public sector work–life balance is 'more rhetoric than reality',[13] and the UK Health and Safety Executive has estimated that the cost to the nation of stress runs into billions of pounds per annum. British men work on average 45 hours a week, with one in three fathers routinely working in excess of 48 hours a week.[14] In the past decade, the number of women working more than 48 hours a week has increased by over 50 per cent. According to the Office for National Statistics, the amount of time spent on voluntary work fell from 2.3 billion hours in 1995 to 1.6 billion hours in 2000; that's a drop of over 30 per cent.[15] According to the Samaritans, people's jobs are the single biggest cause of stress.[16] The Mental Health Foundation says we spend 11 hours a week of our free time thinking about work.[17] In 'burnout Britain', all these organisations imply, many people feel that no one can hear them scream.

THE PROBLEM IS NOT JUST A FEW BAD CORPORATIONS BUT THE ENTIRETY OF LATE-MODERN CAPITALISM

Work experienced as curse is commonplace. And the problem goes deep. 'Work isn't working!' exclaims an anonymous internet article entitled 'Why Freegan?: An Attack on Consumption'.

> Working Sucks – Where does the money you spend come from? You or your folks working long hours at a dehumanizing job, most likely. You don't have to compromise yourself and

> your humanity to the evil demon of wage-slavery! Working sucks and if a little scavenging can keep you from needing a job then go jump in a dumpster! Even if you do need to work to pay your bills, think about how much less you would have to work if you didn't have to buy food.[18]

The New York-based Freegans comprise a movement dedicated to revealing human over-consumption and waste – not least by dropping out of the paid employment economy. After years of trying to boycott products from household-name corporations and finding that no matter what they bought they ended up supporting something deplorable, many Freegans came to realise that the problem is not just a few bad corporations but the entire system itself.[19] Sweatshop labour, rainforest destruction, global warming, displacement of indigenous communities, air and water pollution, eradication of wildlife on farmland, open-pit strip-mining, oil drilling in environmentally sensitive areas, union busting, child slavery, and payoffs to repressive regimes are just some of the many impacts of the seemingly innocuous consumer products we buy every day.

Hence Freeganism's total boycott of an economic system where the profit motive has eclipsed ethical considerations and where massively complex systems of production ensure that the products we buy will have detrimental impacts about which we may never know. Instead of avoiding the purchase of products from one bad company only to support another, they seek to avoid purchasing altogether and hence reduce the amount of paid employment they have to seek.

SOLIDARITY IN SIN

Secularist Freegans are better advocates of Christian teaching about the cursed nature of work and human embroilment in sin than most theologians. 'Man is the least harmless of all beings,' wrote the Jewish teacher and mystic Abraham Heschel.[20] He wrote in allusion to those ungodly death camps where the words *Arbeit Macht Frei* (Work Makes Free) marked the entrance. Today, we do not face the Nazism of the 1930s and 1940s all over again but remain heirs of Adam's curse and the corruption of sin. A Christian ethic of work cannot turn a blind eye to how the West has exported, and is exporting, to developing countries the physical and psychological misery that accompanied its own birth of manufacturing industry, and more besides.

Yet a Christian ethic of work cannot be satisfied with the kind of realism that is so beset by the awfulness of how things are that reasoned and strategic engagement becomes close to impossible. The trouble with unabated realism, says Oliver O'Donovan, is that reasoned, political action can be undermined. Sombre 'realists' are those downcast and shameful in the face of necessity, whose sense of tragedy cuts short 'reasonable interaction' or adequately reasoned engagement with social problems.[21] Christian realists derive truth not only from observation of the things around us but from the event of the resurrection (2 Corinthians 5:1–8) and hope of God's kingdom to come.

The Freegan choice is isolation from the world of work and all its corruption versus collusion with its evils; reasoned, political action for the common good no longer seems either possible or adequate. Too much realism, however, leaves us dispirited and unable to hope. At the other extreme, too much idealism brings its own problems. The trouble with idealism (including theological versions) is that it typically underestimates the complexity of social problems and downplays how conditions, laws and customs differ from one society to another, and ought to differ. 'In the vicious sense of the word', writes O'Donovan, 'it [idealism] supposes some other kind of society, with other problems and possibilities, than the one it actually has to serve.'[22]

A Christian ethic of work derived from the resurrection is not a middle way between realism and idealism. For our purposes, however, the Freegans pose an important challenge. Why not 'opt out' of the workplace? For most of us, the obvious answer is that we simply cannot afford to do so. Yet should 'opting out' be an aspiration for the believer? Should we interpret Jesus' call to leave nets, boats, tax-collecting booth and other means of livelihood as, wherever possible, a call to leave the workplace behind? Should minimal involvement with the multi-national, corporate, air-travelling, energy-guzzling, world of work be the disciple's aim? Should we aspire to a peasant lifestyle of self-sufficiency or new monasticism for the twenty-first century in which a radically simpler lifestyle impacts less harmfully upon our planet?

At one level, the answer must surely be 'yes'. With the Iona Community in Scotland, believers today must surely be committed to seeking new ways of living the gospel that tread lightly upon the earth in terms of environmental damage and carbon footprinting. With the Eco-Congregation movement, we must surely be taking the 'greening' of our houses, churches, workplaces and lifestyles ever more seriously. The ecological crisis is impressing upon us ever more firmly that working more and producing more does not lead to a better quality of life, and that fundamental changes are required in Christian attitudes to the so-called Protestant 'work ethic' and its associations with capitalist ideologies of hard work. For some Christian people, the most effective available witness might even be 'opting out' with the Freegans and/or others of similar persuasion from the solidarity in sin that characterises our workplaces, and how we often spend our wages.

So why not 'opt out' like the Freegans? Why not conclude that the corruption of all things related to work and workplaces is so great that Christian people should separate themselves as much as possible from the damage done by sin? Three reasons present themselves:

1. Amidst our solidarity in sin, the Easter shout of triumph is that the curse of sin is broken. The possibilities available to Christian people are not merely those of 'realism' and 'idealism' (and their diverse associations with failed political projects) but redemption and the hope of transformation by the in-breaking of God's love.
2. The Christian hope of transformation applies to the world(s) of work especially because the curse of sin fell first upon human work. The positioning of the accursed nature

of work in the canon of Holy Scripture is theologically significant because it urges Christians to attribute some kind of priority to present-day socio-political engagement with work.

3. This canonical positioning of the accursed nature of work in the Bible invites Christians to accord priority to socio-political engagement with all matters involving work (e.g. workplace conditions, wages, work–life balance, business ethics, the environmental impact of production and consumption) warrants much more serious attention than is commonly the case. Roman Catholic social teaching is much stronger than Protestant ethics in this respect. Hence we look below at Roman Catholic teaching with respect to work as 'the key to the social question' – albeit with the qualification that much work is needed on the interrelation of issues of social justice and environmental concern.

THINKING WITH THE RESURRECTION

What, then, does it mean to claim that, in Christ, the curse of sin is broken? To the cynic, it might sound like the wishful thinking of a weary man in the Christmas grotto. 'So … apart from a new contract, less bureaucracy, and reduced workloads, is there anything else you want?' asks Santa.[23] Yet the disciple of Christ affirms with St Paul:

> If Christ has not been raised, your faith is futile and you are still in your sins … For since death came through a human being, the resurrection of the dead has also come through a human being; for as all die in Adam, so all will be made alive in Christ. (1 Corinthians 15:17, 21–22)

If Christ has not been raised, our musings about sin as a defeated reality are futile and our best approach to the complex, global problems of work in the twenty-first century is probably Freegan realism. If Christ has not been raised, there is no gospel for the world of work. How, then, are we to understand the gospel for the world(s) of work today?

The answer cannot be that the power of sin as it affects work and workplaces is defeated now in its entirety. Any such claim would fly in the face of empirical observation as alluded to above. Yet the Christian gospel is that the finality of death is removed in Christ, and the curse of sin broken: 'Nothing accursed will be found there any more. But the throne of God and of the Lamb will be in it …' (Revelation 22:3). In the icon of the Harrowing of Hell above, light from Christ's robes extends even to the borders of the icon; the destiny of the entire created order is transfiguration in Christ. Christians live in the light of this hope.

In some versions of the icon Adam's skull and other bones lie adjacent to the broken doors or gates of Hades. Tradition holds that Adam had been held captive deeper down in Hades than all the rest. His release from the very bowels of hell means that nowhere in creation now touched by the curse of sin is beyond Christ's reach. Unlike secularist Freegan realism, Christian *theological realism* is rooted in the reality of the Triune God, 'I am who I am', who transcends the realities of the created order and raised Christ Jesus from the dead.

There is a vitally important interplay, however, between *theological realism* and *political realism*. The theological realism which affirms that Christ is risen and gives hope of liberation from the corruption of sin is no substitute for *political realism* that pays close attention to the day-to-day realities of workplaces and working practices. It is not a question of one or the other. Resurrection presupposes the judgement of crucifixion. Until the coming on earth of God's reign in its fullness, the judgement of crucifixion demands not only that believers live free from the cynicism of unrelieved realism without hope, but that believers are the shrewdest of political realists who bring to sin-ridden workplaces the most probing of questions about self-interest and power, exploitation and oppression, justice and compassion. Disciples of Christ have a different realism from that of the Freegans. With them, however, they want to ask 'who benefits?' and 'who or what pays?'

Two theological truths need to be held together at this point. One is that Christian people are to think and live proleptically, that is, in ways that anticipate God's forthcoming eschatological transformation of this world into the New Jerusalem (Matthew 25:34; Revelation 21:2). The resurrection of Christ is the basis for our hope of transformation. Consequently, we may evaluate the world of human work and participate in its reshaping in light of the promised new creation. In the icon (Figure 2), the mountains reflect the uncreated divine energy, or Taboric light (Matthew 17:2; Mark 9:3; Luke 9:29), that shone from the body of Christ at his transfiguration and resurrection and now reaches every part of the cosmos. The mountains reflect the light which has its source in the resurrected Christ and represent the participation that all creation now has spiritually in divine life and will have more fully at the eschaton.

The other is the continuing need to exercise socio-economic, political and ethical judgement in describing offences against God's law. We need a continuing theological emphasis on God's kingship, law and judgement – not least because a consequence of our own fallen condition is that we cannot guard against corruptibility when filling the eschatological hope of transformation with the content of our own imaginations. Better, says political theologian Oliver O'Donovan, to describe offences against God's law in what he terms 'the ministry of condemnation' than transpose our own prejudices and biases onto the eschatological vision.[24] Hence he calls the Church and/or its representatives to stand against sin exposed by the revealed judgements of God (Revelation 15:4). As a judge does not tell the criminal how to live but passes sentence on the offences committed, so the Church's ministry is not to outline economic policy but to render judgement on actual wrongs, harms done, or that will perhaps be done to future generations. '[I]n an act of political judgment,' says O'Donovan, 'it is the right that is indeterminate, the wrong determined.'[25]

Thinking with the resurrection requires Christian people to hold both truths together simultaneously. So, too, we must hold together issues of social justice and environmental concern. Theological reflection on key concepts and practices in the organisation of workplaces today (e.g. job security, work–life balance, family-friendly policies, job satisfaction and fairness) is scarce. Even scarcer is theological reflection on whether climate change requires 'Western' Christians to prepare ourselves for radical changes in attitude to what we have become accustomed to call 'work'. While the extent of this challenge – as with so many areas of life affected by climate change – is not yet fully evident, responsible Christian theology and ethics must engage with the complexities of new ways of thinking about 'green growth' in relation to issues of social justice. Whilst there has been some interest recently in the academic theological community about work (Gilbert Meilander, Thomas Darrell Cosden, John Hughes), no one has yet rethought the meaning and ethics of work with adequate attention to ecological economics or in ways suggested by liturgical reasoning.

Two further theological truths must also be held together: the cosmic *and* personal scope of the resurrection. Against the backdrop of the unprecedented challenges that global warming is putting to the ways Christian people think about work, the icon of the Harrowing of Hell (Figure 2) teaches clearly that the sacredness of the world cannot be considered apart from the theological and spiritual dimensions of the environment. In this icon of the resurrection, the mountains reflect the light which has its source in the resurrected Christ and represent the participation that all creation has in divine life. In Orthodox iconography of the resurrection, light emanates from Christ's person and his robes, white, pure light. Not even the symbolically rich colour gold is enough to express the glory of God. Only light will do. Victory over the things of hell is disclosed in the whiteness of untouchable light. The rocks which symbolise the entirety of the cosmos reflect the light that has its source in Christ. Consequently, to be called by Christ is to share the light of his presence that brings hope to the entire world.

Yet not only the mountains reflect the uncreated divine light. Keen observers of this icon will note, as Michel Quenot points out, that Adam's sleeve is often much lighter in colour than the rest of his clothing, thereby indicating that a transfiguration or deification is taking place as the scene is filled with the Holy Spirit.[26] Resurrection hope bears directly upon our topic of work and workplaces because the icon includes clear reference to Adam and the chains of sin. Orthodox Christianity has only two icons of the resurrection: the myrrh-bearing women at the tomb and Christ's descent into Hades. Traditional iconography of the latter represents the events of Holy Saturday when Christ himself went to the farthest depths of the fall, to 'that "place" where evil crouches in its ultimate despair' and from where he delivers the great mass of the dead from its darkness. The curse of sin that fell upon Adam and Eve, every aspect of their labour and that of their descendants, is now illumined by the garments of resurrection.

WORK: 'THE KEY TO THE SOCIAL QUESTION'

The phrase 'key to the social question' is taken from Pope John Paul II's 1981 encyclical *Laborem Exercens* (*LE*). This is, arguably, the single most significant theological document to have addressed the topic of work in recent years. It marked the ninetieth anniversary of Pope Leo XIII's Encyclical *Rerum Novarum* (*RN*, 1891) – itself a remarkable text that set a new direction for papal teaching in addressing social issues directly. Briefly stated, *Laborem Exercens* offers a theological conceptuality of work that seeks to recognise the vastness and complexity of the reality of work whilst rooting its teaching in Holy Scripture and tradition, and seeking the ultimate meaning of work in God's gift of creation, the cross and resurrection of Christ.

Despite the canonical positioning and status of questions about work, this kind of prioritising of work in Christian ethics and social engagement is relatively unusual. According to its (most welcome) teaching, fundamental truths about humankind and the nature of work are found in the mystery of creation itself (*LE* §4). Work is a domain of activity where people can imitate what they know of God (*LE* §54) and share in his goodness. Work is neither a curse to be avoided nor merely the route to leisure and/or consumption, not merely something we do to accumulate wealth or facilitate leisure but a fundamental dimension of human existence on earth (*LE* §4) that should be experienced as something worthy that can enhance personal dignity, provide a foundation for family life, and unite people in community. John Paul II's concluding prayer is that the Christian who listens to the word of God and seeks in prayer to subordinate his or her work to the will of God may 'know the place that his work has not only in *earthly progress* but also in *the development of the Kingdom of God*' (*LE* 27).

Today, the most important issues for Christian people struggling with these matters remain those specified by *Laborem Exercens*, namely, what work does *for* people, what work does *to* people, how workers participate in shaping the work experience, and the impact on the poor and powerless who are especially vulnerable and needy.[27] Believers still need to highlight dignity at work as a watchword for Christian engagement with the quality of employment relations. A theological account of work must still grapple with the key insights of recent papal teaching that work is 'the key to the social question' if it is to be effective. The principle that labour is always prior to capital, that is, that people matter more than money or things, must surely remain central to a Christian ethic of work.

Neo-classical economics treats work as one of four essential factors of production (land, labour, entrepreneurship, capital). John Paul II rejects this categorisation by affirming the primacy of human beings and their labour as both the subject and purpose of work (§6). Work is not, he says, to be treated as a 'special kind of "merchandise", or as an impersonal "force" needed for production' (§7); people matter more than money or things. Indeed, *Laborem Exercens* castigates the over-association of 'work' with economic values, affirms the priority of labour over capital, supports the role of trade unions and legally recognised rights of workers as important means of raising labour standards, thereby ensuring that capital, which is a product of labour, serves humans rather than the other way round.

In 1891, *Rerum Novarum* condemned socialism's attempt to do away with private property, which would, it argues, distort the functions of the state (*RN* §4), strike at the interests of every wage-earner (§5), and deny the natural right of private property (§6).[28] Nearly a century later, the greater unease in papal teaching appears to be with the excesses of capitalism. The word 'capitalism', says John Paul II, rightly describes those economic and social systems that subordinate people to the means of production and accumulation of wealth (§7). Such practices threaten the right order of values and must be opposed by the Church. Capital is 'the historical heritage of human labor' (§26). Discord between capital and labour is, however, the central problem of modern societies –

sentiments that, some commentators have argued, sound surprisingly like Marx.[29]

Not surprising, then, that conservative economists were critical when the encyclical was first published. A 1986 lay commission chaired by the strong advocates of *laissez-faire* capitalism William E. Simon and Michael Novak criticised several aspects of *Laborem Exercens*: failure to grasp what made poor nations into richer, developed nations; excessive trust in the state and its officials; an inadequate grasp of crucial concepts such as enterprise and profit.[30] Free-enterprise capitalism tolerates extreme inequality in the workplace for the sake of efficiency and individual freedom.[31]

By contrast, John Paul II saw unrestrained, free-enterprise capital as an evil that must be fought. *Laborem Exercens* uses the term 'exploitation' frequently, as does the later encyclical *Sollicitudo Rei Socialis* (*SRS*, 1987) which deals with global economic development. 'From the beginning of the industrial age', writes John Paul II, 'the Christian truth about work had to oppose the various trends of *materialistic* and *economistic* thought' (*LE* §7). The Church has no model of the best economic system to present (*Centesimus Annus* §43) and should not go outside her own specific field of competence, still less outside the mandate received from the Lord (*SRS* §8). The Church's social doctrine is not a 'third way' between free-enterprise, or liberal, capitalism and Marxist collectivism; 'it constitutes a category of its own' (*SRS* §41). Even so, the Church condemns the evils and injustices of workplaces that treat human labour solely according to its economic purpose and urges 'motivating concern' for 'the Lord's poor' (*SRS* §43).[32]

Historians of Roman Catholic social teaching tell us that this emphasis on the personal aspect of labour as the basis for the priority of labour over capital is a mid-to-late twentieth-century phenomenon. The most common emphases in nineteenth-century Roman Catholic teaching were natural and divine law, human nature and the importance of order in human affairs, *not* the quality of human relationships or the extent of personal moral responsibilities. Sceptics who try to decode papal teaching suggest that the change in emphasis was the result of a change in 'opponent' from economic liberalism with its Enlightenment notions of freedom from authoritarian religion to totalitarianism – whether fascism, nazism or communism.

In other words, the agenda underlying the move towards what is sometimes called Catholic personalism was bound up with papal opposition to Marxism. According to Charles E. Curran, Pope John XXIII's *Pacem in Terris* in 1963 signalled the Catholic acceptance of the role of freedom and, more particularly, the role of human rights in protecting individual freedom. By 1981, the focus was the Marxists still functioning in Eastern Europe and the liberation theologians in Latin America.[33] John Paul II adopted just enough Marxist critique of capitalism to take away their moral initiative and to capture the moral high ground of human rights and concern for the poor. Individual freedom and dignity are now the focus of attention rather than order and social cohesiveness.[34]

Despite the messiness and compromise of Vatican politics as exposed by historians, however, *Laborem Exercens* teaches clearly that the gospel of Christ has consequences for how we think about work. In closing this chapter, I want to acknowledge the massive contribution of *Laborem Exercens* to ecumenical Christian ethics in putting the treatment of labour centre stage in the creation of just societies and placing work higher up the theological agenda.

Chapter 3

RESURRECTION AND LITURGICAL MORAL REASONING

> A song for occupations!
> In the labor of engines and trades and the labor of fields I find the developments,
> And find the eternal meanings.
> House-building, measuring, sawing the boards,
> Blacksmithing, glass-blowing, nail-making, coopering, tin-roofing, shingle-dressing,
> Ship-joining, dock-building, fish-curing, flagging of sidewalks by flaggers,
> The pump, the pile-driver, the great derrick, the coal-kiln and brickkiln,
> Coal-mines and all that is down there, the lamps in the darkness, echoes, songs, what meditations ...[1]

One of the central assertions of this chapter is that the meaning and ethics of work is learned, at least in part, from the Church's practice of worship. Here we learn best to interpret Holy Scripture and, arguably, perceive most clearly the logic or reasoning that is to determine our thinking about work. Here we grasp that all our work – whether that of the health-care giver or the patient whose work for a period is to receive care – finds its proper destiny in God's drama of redemption. The work of the worshipping people of God is one of the best available vehicles for thinking through questions of social ethics.

Liturgies vary, of course, from tradition to tradition. Yet the basic grammar of Christian liturgy, its fixed elements, narratives, concepts and practices, are common across traditions. Our personal experience of Christian worship might be context-bound and local but the inclusiveness and universality of the sacraments have a transcendent quality that exceeds our particularity. We work with the following shape of most eucharistic liturgies:

1. *Gathering* – coming together of the people for worship;
2. *Anaphora* – offering up of the world to God in thanksgiving, assuming on theological grounds the proper autonomy of the 'secular';
3. *Anamnesis* – remembering of Christ's passion, not in a way to make secular disciplines rivals to the Church but to be oriented by spiritual goals whilst still allowing other disciplines to inform the prophetic clarity of theological critique;
4. *Epiclesis* – invocation of God's Holy Spirit for strength to transform the perceptible world and, where appropriate, to seek to change the many agendas of other disciplines, public and/or societal life;
5. *Communion* – repentance as moment of simple truth amidst multiple complexity; sacrifice as integral to reconciliation and healing; anticipatory consummation of the unity of all things in God;
6. *Dismissal* – sending of persons back to their many walks of life, and to the relative autonomy of respective disciplines and/or workplaces.

This classical shape of the liturgy is described in minimally different form by Dom Gregory Dix in his famous *The Shape of the Liturgy* (1945). He concentrates on the offering (*anaphora*), that is, the 'taking' of bread and wine in a form that was derived probably from the Jewish *chaburah* meal; the prayer of thanksgiving, derived from the *berakah* or prayer which closed the *chaburah* meal; the breaking of bread, derived from the Jewish grace before all meals; and the communion or eating of the bread and drinking of the cup of blessing.[2] These differences are of minimal, if any, significance. So, for instance, I include thanksgiving in the movement of *anaphora*. What matters more than the particular moments emphasised is why the structure of the liturgy has remained in this standard shape and how it bears upon our thinking.

Liturgical reasoning is not exclusively Christian. All of the Abrahamic faiths find meaning in liturgical worship because this is where the relationship between God, his Word and the world is experienced with special intensity. The liturgy is, as it were, the language that all the faiths speak. Liturgy, says Jewish scholar Steven Kepnes, 'is like a language with semiotic conventions that have to be mastered', that is, the study of signs or symbols.[3] His book *Jewish Liturgical Reasoning* talks about attending carefully 'to the systems of language and discourse that underlie and are used within monotheistic liturgies'.[4] From his perspective, liturgical reasoning offers an immensely rich way of thinking and exploring how God's dwelling with his people continually discloses new dimensions of meaning, philosophical conceptions of truth, and directions for ethical action. His work is about describing the dynamic of Jewish worship and seeking through the corporate practice of worship to discern the application of Torah to everyday life. Written Torah, he says, provides the words, or basic units of vocabulary and thought, for leading a faithful Jewish life. The liturgy or worshipping life of the people is where to search for the hermeneutical rules, or ways of interpreting Torah, that will guide one day by day.

LITURGICAL REASONING

So, how does liturgical reasoning work? There is no easy description! But think about a church service that you might have attended recently, a hymn that you sang, or even a conversation with a friend, during which you attained a little more clarity about how to approach a problem or situation. So, for instance, I sang the hymn 'My song is love unknown' recently. It caused me somehow to think of an elderly lady for whom this hymn was a great favourite, and spurred me into writing her a letter the next day. Or consider the preacher who comments on how members of a congregation make the most unexpected connections between the sermon preached and their personal circumstances. 'Sometimes', a preacher said to me recently, 'I barely recognise the sermon that I am supposed to have preached.' Liturgical reasoning is about the kind of connections between the sermon and the thoughts or decisions of the congregation.

The sceptic might talk at this point about day-dreaming or mere musings. It's all a bit vague. Why should such informal plays of thought be accorded the high status of 'reasoning'? Can it really be that a businessman's decision which crystallised in his mind, whilst half-listening to a sermon, bore any reasoned relation to the doctrinal content of the sermon? The sermon was not about money or the workplace, morality or decision-making. Why, then, did its content direct him toward deciding to refuse the contract? Liturgical reasoning is interested in this kind of issue. Why and how, the liturgical reasoner asks, does worship, and the liturgy especially, become a vehicle of social ethics for believers? How might the truths enacted in the liturgy permeate, shape and colour the attitudes of believers towards everyday work and diverse moral concerns? Not satisfied with merely deductive (top-down) and inductive (bottom-up) modes of reasoning, liturgical reasoning remains close to the worshipping people(s) of God, and learns from what seems to happen in the lives of the faithful.

It is important to make plain that the phrase 'liturgical reasoning' and, indeed, the practice of liturgical reasoning, has been associated in recent years with the pioneering work of Steven Kepnes (mentioned above) and Peter Ochs, another Jewish scholar based at the University of Virginia, USA. Drawing on the internal patterns of reasoning evident in synagogue liturgies and the pragmatic philosophy of C. S. Peirce respectively, these scholars have done more than any others recently to explain this mode of reasoning and unpack its significance for communities of faith. Why is it, wonders Peter Ochs, for instance, that the minds of believers select from innumerable stimuli to reach certain inferences? What goes on in our proto-logic or pre-critical 'thinking' that leads us to certain hypotheses?

In logic, philosophers often talk about deductive and inductive methods of reasoning. Deduction moves from general or universal premises to conclusions about particulars. Induction infers general conclusions from particular instances. To explain further, I borrow Peter Ochs' description of abduction, in contrast with deduction and induction, as follows.[5] So, for instance, deduction may be typified by the syllogism:

> All men are mortal;
> Socrates is a man;
> therefore Socrates is mortal.

Induction is typified by the syllogism:

> This person is mortal and a human;
> that person is mortal and a human;
> therefore we conclude that all humans may be mortal.

Christian ethics can be done in similar ways. So, for instance, a deductive approach may be sketched as follows:

> All persons are loved by God;
> Tyra is a person;
> therefore Tyra is loved by God.

Alternatively:

> God commands his people to love their neighbours as themselves;
> Susan is my neighbour;
> therefore I must love her as God commands.

This deductive approach to Christian ethics seeks to move from the commands of God, or confession of Christ crucified and risen, to the concerns of everyday life. The problem is that it rarely gets there. It is not clear how to make the connections. Sometimes additional principles are abstracted from Holy Scripture to function as intermediate guidelines between the texts and everyday situations. Principles such as 'the priority of the poor' sometimes float between the universality of God's commands in Scripture and concrete, material situations. The problem is knowing how to put the principle into practice.

By contrast, an inductive approach may be outlined as follows:

> This person is out of work and poor;
> that person is out of work and poor;
> therefore we conclude that all people who are out of work are poor.

So, for instance, feminist theologians sometimes urge readers to reflect upon their experience and move from it to some general conclusions or theories. The problem is that the limitations of one's own experiences and subjectivity may skew one's 'take' on the problem.

Abductive reasoning is an alternative to inductive and deductive logic. It is, its advocates suggest, a more open, multi-staged method than inductive and deductive reasoning, and is open to other possible ways of reaching a conclusion. Not all of the steps and processes entailed in deductive reasoning are likely to be trustworthy, nor do they always lead to a practical conclusion. Similarly, the conclusions reached by inductive reasoning might be unduly influenced by personal experience and cultural bias. Neither 'top-down' nor 'bottom-up' may be relied upon as likely to yield a robust result. Abductive reasoners recognise the limitations associated with inductive and deductive reasoning and attempt to take seriously the fallible nature of our reasoning and how our context or 'situatedness' bears upon our thinking processes. So, for instance, abductive reasoning may be typified as follows:

> We know that squirrels climb trees and eat nuts.
> Now, I see a little creature climbing a tree and eating a nut;
> perhaps it's a squirrel.[6]

Upon seeing the squirrel, our selective pre-conscious is flooded with stimuli. Memories and snippets of knowledge are present to us in pre-rational form. Amidst these many stimuli and from a variety of pre-critical inferences, however, we characterise what we see as 'perhaps or probably a squirrel'. From a range of possibilities, we arrive at a certain hypothesis that can then be tested inductively. Abduction is, says Ochs, integral to how we formulate hypotheses. Scriptural or liturgical reasoning is, at its most basic, an investigation of abductive reasoning amongst communities of believers.

So, for instance, believers might reason as follows:

> We know from the Bible that the poor have a special place in the heart of God.
> I also know that unemployment tends to bring poverty.
> Perhaps the members of the Church should do something to bring the love of God to the unemployed.

Abductive reasoning entails both the selection and formation of hypotheses. Abduction is, says Ochs, a way of thinking that is suited especially to believers engaged reading Scripture and performing the liturgy.[7] Believers whose lives are shaped by repetitive readings of Holy Scripture and the familiar actions of the liturgy select from their knowledge and experience to form hypotheses about right action. Whereas deduction tries to prove coherent links between premises and conclusions, and induction seeks a probable generalisation that arises coherently from premises and experience, abduction can reason in both of these directions according to what the reasoner's best efforts and instincts deem necessary.

This might sound vague. Indeed, the process is vague and fallible. But no one is claiming to get it right all the time. More importantly, says Ochs, abductive reasoning describes the kinds of connections that people make between sermons, or hymns, or the liturgy, and their everyday affairs. We may not understand the processes entailed in any precise ways. Yet these connections happen and may be said to constitute a form of reasoning. It is a fallible form of reasoning. Yet all human reasoning is fallible. Advocates of abductive reasoning take seriously the fallibility of human reasoning, whether as individuals or a community, and build recognition of fallibility into their attempts to make sense of how humans reason. The challenge for liturgical reasoners is to make some sense of how believers derive guidance (or understand how others have derived guidance) for ethical thinking from the liturgy, hymn singing, praying and, of course, the reading and exploration of Holy Scripture – all of which are integral to liturgical worship.

The irony is that, typically, liturgical reasoning is done only poorly through books of this kind! Think again, however, about the businessman for whom a decision about whether or not to accept a contract crystallised in his mind whilst half-listening to a sermon, or the radiographer uncertain about whether to report a colleague for turning up drunk to work, or the chief executive concerned about the growing gap between the salaries of cleaners, janitors and other service workers as compared to the managers and high-grade specialists.

Little, if anything, in the Bible or liturgy per se speaks directly to these issues. Yet Christians believe that Holy Scripture is still 'sufficient to declare the truth' in matters of both doctrine and morals.[8] The substance or stuff of the Bible is written by human hands and thus creaturely.[9] Yet Christians believe it to be a means of grace with a special place in God's saving dealings with humankind from which guidance may be obtained for even the most minor of day-to-day concerns. 'All scripture is inspired by God and is useful for teaching, reproof, for correction, and for training in righteousness, so that everyone who belongs to God may be proficient, equipped for every good service' (2 Timothy 3:16–17). Talk about *using* the Bible in ethics is already a distortion. The Bible is not an object or a tool for us to use as we choose. How, then, do the Holy Scripture, the practice of worship, meeting in fellowship, and other such activities, bear upon the day-to-day concerns of believers?

Peter Ochs' exposition of liturgical reasoning offers a useful way of thinking about this question. He describes liturgical reasoning by means of what he calls A-Reasonings and B-Reasonings. A-Reasonings are *foundational* to the life of the given community as, for instance, biblical accounts of the LORD's call of Abraham or the Exodus from Egypt are foundational to Jewish identity, and the resurrection of Christ from the dead is the truth upon which the Church is built.[10] B-Reasonings include one's personal or societal background and experience, inferences drawn from these experiences, and observations on what is going on in the world. Both may be unreliable and/or vague. Some believers might have scant knowledge of their tradition. Few members of a given community will have tried to articulate their A-Reasonings fully. B-Reasonings are always subject to revision in the light of changed circumstances. Moreover, that we come from different backgrounds and traditions, have different experiences of poverty, wealth and class, are variously disabled, gendered and aged, and otherwise think differently, is likely to bear upon our decision-making.

Abduction, says Ochs, is what happens when B-Reasonings come into contact with A-Reasonings. In other words, abduction happens when something in everyday life (B-Reasonings) provokes us to call upon those foundational truths and/or practices (A-Reasonings) that have sustained us hitherto. The process is fallible, always fallible. *All* human reasoning is fallible and subject to correction. For believers, however, Holy Scripture and the liturgy are the sources from which we draw our means for making sense of the world, our purpose for living, our guidelines for moral decision-making, and so on. Abduction is a logic of relationship; not simply the ideas with which our heads might be buzzing but, at its best, a communal practice in which we engage with one another to identify overlapping assumptions and/or justifications for a course of action. Abduction may, says Ochs, be called insight or the emergence of an explanatory or constructive hypothesis from the mix of questions, biblical teaching, social context, emotional strains and liturgical practice, that has made us what we are today.

Mindful, then, that abduction is a relational phenomenon that is likely to involve many people and is best done in contexts of friendship, trust, mutual support and questioning, our aim in the remainder of this chapter is to attempt to allow it to happen. Abduction is a tricky subject to write about because, as Ochs (following C. S. Peirce) says, it only yields suggestions.[11] It does not yield a theory or steps in a coherent argument but belongs to the class of operations to which perceptual judgement belongs. Favourable character references might say of a person that they typically exercise sound judgement. Examples might be given of when they were shown to have been wise, prudent or such like. It is probably not possible, however, to specify in any detail the steps that this person takes in their deliberations. There is no guaranteed route to insight or wise judgement. Similarly, there is no guarantee of the wisdom yielded by abductive reasoning. What follows are my own insights with respect to work that have arisen in the context of the liturgy.

THE GATHERING OF THE PEOPLE

Firstly, the liturgy helps us to *think together* about issues of social justice and environmental concern. This is evident especially in aspects of the liturgy relating to the gathering of the people. In the work of worship, one's personal work of paid employment or other means of livelihood and, indeed, the activities of the week more generally, cannot be separated from their cosmic and eternal context. In the liturgy, one's personal work cannot be separated from the wider context of the entire created order. In the liturgy, work is not merely something that I do but something that brings me into relationship with others of God's creatures, throughout this generation and in those to come.

In the Orthodox liturgy, the people sing Psalm 103 as they gather for worship: 'Bless the Lord, O my soul', the people exhort one another, and the psalm continues:

> and do not forget all his benefits –
> who forgives all your iniquity,
>   who heals all your diseases,
> who redeems your life from the Pit,
>   who crowns you with steadfast love and mercy,
> who satisfies you with good as long as you live
>   so that your youth is renewed like the eagle's.
>
> The LORD works vindication
>   and justice for all who are oppressed.
> He made known his ways to Moses,
>   his acts to the people of Israel.

Gratitude for God's goodness in creation is reinforced by gratitude for the life, death and resurrection of Jesus Christ. The people of Israel sang the praises of the LORD God who redeemed them from slavery. Christians proclaim the same God who redeems from sin and continues to bestow renewing gifts of grace on all creation. In the Orthodox liturgy, the deacon moves to stand before an icon of Christ just after the opening anthems and before the litanies or prayers of supplication, summoning the people to praise the God revealed in Jesus Christ. The people gather both in memory of God's work of salvation and in anticipation of the day when every creature in heaven and on earth and under the earth and in the sea will sing glory to the one seated on the throne and to the lamb (Revelation 5:13).

In the Divine Liturgy of St John Chrysostom, the Great Litany at the beginning of the service includes prayers for the peace of the whole world, the unity of all the churches of God, the country, the president, and all those in public office, the parish and city, every city and country, for travellers by land, sea and air, for the sick and the suffering and those in captivity, and more besides. The context in which the faithful gather is global and local, familiar and unfamiliar, immediate and transgenerational. The First Antiphon (sentence sung by one group in expectation of response from another) urges all the faithful to pray to the Lord for mercy and protection. The prayer is offered not only for the congregation and their families but for the world in its entirety: the earth is the Lord's! 'Save Your people and bless Your inheritance.' Later, at the Litany of Fervent Supplication, prayers are offered again for the country, its ruler, its people, civil authorities and armed forces, the bishop and clergy, devout kings and right-believing queens, and more besides – the reason being that God is merciful and loves humankind.

The liturgy unfolds to disclose levels of interconnection between persons across the world and across the generations. A Methodist service from my own tradition suggests the following prayer for early in the service: 'Generous God, You gave your Son for the life of the whole world. Give us the joy of knowing the risen Christ …' Rooting an ethic of work here requires believers to abandon modern, liberal notions of our work as a 'private affair' that should be as free from the interference of others as is possible within the constraints of a democratic society. Rather than work being something done by an individual for their own sake and that of their family, liturgical worship requires us to think about work differently. Participation in the liturgy requires us to begin from, not move toward, an understanding of work as worship and work as relationship.

The sceptic might object at this point that work is essentially private because, typically, it entails contractual relations between individuals or between individuals and corporations, and because individual workers' interests are variously protected at law. The very essence of paid employment, the sceptic might assert, is that it allocates to individuals some measure of control over the use of their time and acquisition of property. Employers expect some degree of exclusivity in the benefits that accrue from their employees' endeavours. In return, employees enjoy a measure of exclusivity in the enjoyment of the wages earned and other benefits accrued. And, in a limited sense, the sceptic is correct. Most paid employment entails a contract of some kind between individuals and/or corporations. My point is not to deny this obvious reality about employment relationships but draw attention to how learning an ethic of work from worship draws our attention to matters other than the merely individual and contractual. In the cosmic and eternal context of worship, our everyday activity in the workplace intersects in many ways with the lives of others.

Modern notions of the private–public divide are rarely adequate to describe the interconnectedness of the created order. Taglines for the film *Babel* include: 'A single gunshot heard around the world' and 'One shot, many kills'.[12] The film tells four seemingly distinct stories but interconnected stories – a troubled couple on vacation in Morocco trying to work through their differences, a Moroccan herder whose sons play with a rifle that he bought to keep jackals away from his herd, a Mexican nanny taking the couple's two children with her to her son's wedding in Mexico, and a girl in Japan dealing with the death of her mother and her own emerging sexuality. The whole point of the film is to describe how, as humans, we find ourselves today: scattered across the face of the globe in various states of division, dislocation, inability to communicate, and confusion. The complexities of global markets, increasing interconnectivity of economic decisions, technological innovations, cultural tensions, and political struggles around the world, mean that people of many languages and cultures do not understand one another's speech. In such contexts, the meaning of work as learned in worship expands our ethic of work from what we do as individuals to the multiple interconnections that our various activities entail.

Anaphora: offering up of the world to God

In this section we turn to the offering up to God of the bread and wine in thanksgiving. In the Orthodox liturgy, the priest says: 'Thy gifts of what is Thine, do we offer to Thee, in all we do and for all Thy Blessings.' In a variant translation, it reads: 'We offer to You these gifts from Your own gifts in all and for all.'[13] Similarly, in the Methodist Service of Holy Communion during Ordinary Seasons (First Service), bread and wine are brought to the table (or uncovered) and the Minister says:

> Lord and Giver of every good thing, we bring to you bread and wine for our communion, lives and gifts for your kingdom, all for transformation through your grace and love, made known in Jesus Christ our Saviour. Amen.

Both services include a paradoxical offering to God of what is not really ours; presenting to God what is already his.

What, then, of our work is taken and offered by the priest or minister at the Eucharist? The people of Israel were to bring only the 'first fruits' to the Lord (Exodus 22:29–31; Leviticus 23:15–21; Deuteronomy 22:9; Numbers 18:27). The book of the prophet Malachi (1:11) speaks of a 'pure offering'. Today, churches use anything from wafer-like hosts, home-made rolls, slices from a mass-produced shop-bought loaf, to whatever the local bakery has left on a Saturday afternoon. When offered at the altar or table, however, it ceases to be merely the bread purchased or made by the members. The bread offered is not common bread, it is not merely bread made at home or bought locally, but becomes for the faithful a reality composed of two realities, an earthly and a heavenly. The Eucharist (literally 'thanksgiving') is the mystery in which bread and wine made by human hands become for us the body and blood of Christ. Eating and drinking this food is not important for satisfying physical hunger or thirst but is necessary for eternal life. This is why, says Dom Gregory Dix, the earliest Christians taught that bodies receiving the Eucharist are 'no more corruptible, having the hope of eternal resurrection'.[14]

The *anaphora* cannot be explained merely in terms of the priest or minister offering to God bread and wine that represents the world as we know it. As 'common bread', that is, the world and its work as we know it, this offering is not worthy of God's presence but subject to judgement and wrath. Yet, in his providential involvement in human history, God has chosen to act through loaves or bread and the work of humans. The bread offered *is* common: it comes from and represents our everyday lives. It was bought with our wages or money from our pension, made by hand or mass-produced in a factory, and sold at a profit. When offered to God, however, a dynamic other than the merely human comes into play. By grace, the bread offered is sanctified through its incorporation into the resurrection of Christ. The world as we know it, in its 'Babel' state, and from which the bread came, is offered to God and made holy by incorporation into the life divine (1 Corinthians 10:16).

Bread from the local bakery represents what I am calling the proper autonomy of the secular. The secular is what belongs to this age or is part of the historical order that we all inhabit. Offering this bread to God, in the knowledge that the divine life will infuse its every part, becomes the framework in which to think about the work of all human hands. The eschatological, forward-looking dynamic of the Eucharist gives meaning not only to the bread but to the work of all human hands. Recall again the words of the prayer, 'Lord and Giver of every good thing ...', quoted above. The *anaphora* can be a prayer that all human labour will bear fruit for the final consummation of God's purpose.

At the *anaphora*, the focus is the saving work of God. Contemplation of the grace of God in redemption calls forth a prayer from the people that everything in all creation be offered to God in Christ, taken up and transformed. Praise and intercession may be distinguished but cannot be separated from each other, or from other moments in the Eucharist. Nor can the meditative and mental aspects of prayer be separated from the affective and contemplative. Concerns about workplaces that belong to the proper autonomy of the secular are drawn into the transforming influence of the gospel. As bread made by human hands is offered for the feast, the prayers of the people cannot but include intercessions arising from the many domestic and work environments of which we have experience. The dynamic is not that the needs of the world are a stimulus to intercession – this approach to intercession tends to result in exhaustion and despair. Rather, the *anaphora* centres our attention upon God's purposes of blessing for all creation.

Deductive reasoning at this point would attempt to exhibit the meaning of this belief by moving from general or universal premises to conclusions about particulars. There would, of course, be great value in a study of this kind – perhaps with respect to what it means to say that the Spirit of Christ reaches into the lives of every believer who eats the eucharistic bread. Inductive reasoning would evaluate the truth of these claims by identifying the relation between the belief in question (e.g., that the believer participates in the life of Christ and thereby enjoys the filial relation enjoyed between God the Father and God the Son) and the difference that it makes in the lives of communicants to affirm this belief. Theo-logic would be employed in recognised and helpful, if somewhat formulaic, ways.

Abductive reasoning might yield something more like the following:

I know that the bread in the hands of the priest came from the local bakery.
I believe that God will receive it and transform it for me into Christ's flesh which he gives for the life of the world (John 6:51).
Perhaps not only the loaf but also the labour that produced it is transformed by the Spirit when lifted toward the cross of Christ.

Abductive reasoning, the kind of reasoning that often happens in the hearts and minds of believers when they are not really trying to think in an orderly manner but allowing connections to become evident, allows seemingly unrelated facts to find points of contact. In this example, connections are made between the labour employed at a local business and the actions of the minister or priest in lifting up the bread in dedication. At the least, the meaning of work as learned abductively in worship expands our perceptions of work from what we do day by day as individuals to the multiple interconnections that our various activities entail.

ANAMNESIS: REMEMBERING CHRIST'S PASSION

'Shabbat gives a "taste of redemption".'[15] This, says Jewish scholar Steven Kepnes, is what the rabbis teach. Shabbat, that is, the Sabbath, makes believers hungry for the realisation of justice. Observance of Shabbat is how Jews learn the meaning of justice and acquire the passion that energises action for social change.

Here is the nub of the matter. The taste of Christ's passion makes the Christian hungry for social justice. Active remembrance of Christ's passion, that is, participation in the eucharistic life of the Church, is not merely recollection of the events of Holy Week. Participants at the Eucharist remember Christ's passion not as we remember a family birthday last month or the day we graduated from college but as that which draws us into the very life of God. Believers not only recall but partake of 'all that came to pass for our sake, the cross, the tomb, the resurrection on the third day, the ascension into heaven, the enthronement at the right hand of the

Father, and the second, glorious coming': 'The Lamb of God is broken and distributed; broken but not divided. He is forever eaten yet is never consumed, but He sanctifies those who partake of Him.'[16]

Believers not only remember but share in the benefits of the one sacrifice of Christ, in all its completion and inclusiveness; in the pardoning of sins and instilling in our hearts of the assurance of resurrection. This sharing in the benefits of redemption makes the believer hungry for the fulfilment of God's work of love to restore humankind to its vocation of union and communion with God (2 Corinthians 3:18; 2 Peter 1:4), and to heal and renew the cosmos (Romans 8:21; Revelation 21:5). When one begins to have a conceptual awareness that Christ's victory over death and sin has implications for our world of the promise of God's reign, one becomes aware of the inclusion of humankind in the divine work of love to restore and renew all things – not least the accursed nature of work.

'Bring it on!' the believer might say. We know the accursed nature of work. But we also know that Christ is risen. We know God's means of dealing with sin and its consequences, and of elevating creation to the blessing that was prepared before the fall into sin (Psalm 103:19; Isaiah 64:4; Romans 9:23). Redemption is not yet complete; it is a movement toward the future in which the whole earth will be healed, restored, and transformed (Isaiah 44:24–28; Romans 1:16, 8:23, 13:11; Ephesians 4:30). 'His intrinsically perfect work is still moving towards its consummation.'[17] We yearn for the day when workplaces are free of exploitation, when the needs of all are met, when the paradisal or blessed nature of work is restored. Until that day, the taste for redemption acquired at the Eucharist sensitises our palate to the flavour of God's justice and makes us hungry for more.

The imagery of taste, flavour and aroma can be pushed too far. Yet consider Aaron Bacall's cartoon of two cheery-looking executives in conversation as they stroll out of their office building. 'The company is doing much better', says one to the other, 'since we outsourced our ethics division to tribal warlords.'[18] In the vacuum left by the erosion of traditional and religious approaches to ethics, their ethical needs could be met by a range of suppliers. The supplier they chose turned upon whether or not they liked the product. The ethical tastes of these executives are sensitive to the smell of success and whiff of profit. The combination of ruthless competition and dominance with respect to market share leads them to prefer the ethics of tribal warlords.

The taste of redemption acquired at Shabbat is not, says Steven Kepnes, exclusively for personal enjoyment – though this is a feature of the experience. Rather, the witness of the prophets is that divine judgement and redemption will stretch to the corners of the globe (Isaiah 11:12, 41:1–2; Jeremiah 9:26). The prophetic hope of redemption is never impersonal or atemporal. Philosophical ideas of justice may be atemporal. The witness of the prophets is that redemption becomes temporalised wherever a neighbour is in need or a workplace accursed. Remembrance of Christ's passion is a yearning for the inbreaking of God's reign, a hunger for all creation to be reborn, a remembrance of the future.

Christian action for justice is *not* comparable in kind to Christ's work on the cross. Paul wrote to the Colossians (if, indeed, Paul was the author of this letter) that his sufferings filled up (Greek from *antanaplēroō* meaning 'filled up in turn') the sufferings of Christ (Colossians 1:24–29). The prefix *ant-* before *anaplēroō* conveys a sense of exchange or something given in return for an action on Christ's part. Paul's 'completing what is lacking in Christ's afflictions for the sake of his body' does not compromise the *ephapax* (once for all) nature of Christ's sacrifice on Golgotha (Romans 6:10; Hebrews 7:27, 9:12, Greek *ephapax*). Christ's action is not to be repeated, yet Paul and the Church have work to do in human history because the work of redemption is not yet complete.

The construction of the word from '*epi*' (over or above) and '*hapax*' (once) is emphatic; Christ died to sin *once and for all*. No 'ifs' or 'buts'. No qualification needed. Priests at the altar do not repeat Christ's sacrifice. The blood of goats and calves isn't any longer required because, by his own blood, he entered once into the holy of holies, having obtained eternal redemption for us all. There is no question in these texts but that Christ's death on the cross was comprehensive and for all time. It includes all time and people: 'it is by God's will that we have been sanctified through the offering of the body of Jesus Christ once for all' (Hebrews 10:10). Nothing that we do bears upon this *once for all* nature of the work of the cross.[19]

The Orthodox scholar Protopresbyter Michael Pomazansky says it as well as anyone: 'The Eucharistic sacrifice *is not a repetition* of the Saviour's sacrifice on the Cross, but it is an offering of the sacrificed Body and Blood offered once by our Redeemer on the Cross, by Him Who "is ever eaten, though never consumed".'[20] The Eucharist is a bloodless passion in the sense that it is performed after the resurrection. 'We know that Christ, being raised from the dead, will never die again; death no longer has dominion over him' (Romans 6:10). Yet believers become *presently operative* in the ongoing work or the cross. The foretaste of the heavenly banquet prepared for all people gives participants at the Eucharist a taste for what they know to be right. Anamnesis of the passion is perpetually creative of both the corporate life of the Church and the hunger for justice.[21]

Epiclesis: invocation of God's Holy Spirit

Epiclēsis means to call upon (Greek *epi* meaning upon + *kaleō* which means to call, summon). In the Divine Liturgy of St John Chrysostom, the priest blesses the bread with the words:

> Once again we offer to You this spiritual worship without the shedding of blood, and we ask, pray, and entreat You: send down Your Holy Spirit upon us and upon these gifts here presented ...
> And make this bread the precious Body of Your Christ.

He then blesses the cup which contains the wine, the precious blood of Christ, and says in a low voice:

> Changing them by your Holy Spirit.
> Amen. Amen. Amen.[22]

Shortly following this prayer that the body and blood of Christ may, by the power of the Holy Spirit, become for participants the reality in their lives of the forgiveness of sins, communion with the Holy Spirit, confidence that they stand not in judgement and condemnation, the priest offers prayers of intercession for the city in which they live, and every city and country, the faithful who dwell therein, the sick, the suffering, the captives, those who do charitable work, those who care for the poor, and all other human concerns.

Similarly, the Litany of *The Book of Common Prayer* (1662) calls upon the Holy Spirit to bless and preserve the people as they seek justice, peace, and the general good of the society:

> That it may please thee to bless and keep the Magistrates, giving them grace to execute justice, and to maintain truth;
> *We beseech thee to hear us, good Lord.*
>
> That it may please thee to bless and keep all thy people,
> *We beseech thee to hear us, good Lord.*
>
> That it may please thee to give to all nations unity, peace, and concord,
> *We beseech thee to hear us, good Lord.*
>
> That it may please thee to give us an heart to love and dread thee, and diligently to live after thy commandments,
> *We beseech thee to hear us, good Lord.*
>
> That it may please thee to give to all thy people increase of grace, to hear meekly thy Word, and to receive it with pure affection, and to bring forth the fruits of the Spirit,
> *We beseech thee to hear us, good Lord.*

My plea is for new litanies and variety in our formal prayers so that we pray explicitly for workplaces, relationships at work, the end of exploitation, living wages, fair working practices, the home or charity shop as a workplace, and other such concerns.

The following is adapted from a prayer written by Kenneth Fernandes.[23]

Heavenly Father, as we enter our work places this week, we take Your presence with us. We pray for Your peace, Your grace, Your mercy and Your perfect order, wherever our work takes us this week. We acknowledge Your power over all that will be spoken, thought, decided and done.

Lord, we thank You for the gifts You have blessed us with. We commit to using them responsibly in Your honour. Give us a fresh supply of strength to do our job. Anoint our projects, ideas and energy so that even our smallest accomplishments may bring You glory.

Lord, when we are confused, guide us. When we are weary, energize us. When we are burned out, infuse us with the light of the Holy Spirit. May the work that we do and the way we do it bring faith, joy and a smile to all with whom we come in contact this week.

And Oh Lord, when we leave for work in the mornings, give us travelling mercy. Bless our families and homes to remain in order as we left them. Lord we thank You for everything You've done, everything You're doing, and everything You're going to do.

In the mighty Name of Jesus we pray, with love and thanksgiving ...
Amen.

This next prayer is called 'A prayer for Fridays'. Its simple adaptation of Isaiah 58:6–7, 10 comes from the Archdiocese of Chicago:[24]

This is the fast that pleases me:
  to break unjust fetters,
to let the oppressed go free,
  to share your bread with the hungry
and shelter the homeless poor.
  If you do away with the yoke,
the clenched fist, the wicked word,

if you give your bread to the hungry
and relief to the oppressed,
your light will rise in the darkness.
Isaiah 58:6–7, 10

The following prayer could be focused by anyone upon the responsibilities of the day:

> Dear Lord, I give you my hands to do Your work [in *name of place* today];
> I give You my feet to go Your way [as I walk into *name of place* today];
> I give You my eyes to see as You see [as I expect to see *name of person* today];
> I give You my tongue to speak Your words [as I prepare for *name of presentation or meeting*];
> I give You my mind that You may think in me [particularly with respect to *name of challenge*];
> I give You my spirit that You may pray in me.
> Above all, I give You my heart that You may love in me – love the Father and love all humankind.
> I give You my whole self, Lord, that You may grow in me, so that it is You who lives, works and prays in me. Amen.[25]

Dismissal

The dismissal, or sending of persons back to their many walks of life, and to the relative autonomy of respective disciplines, is a vitally important part of the liturgy. Some ministers ask the congregation to turn toward the door by which they will leave as he or she utters the words of blessing. This symbolises that God's Spirit will accompany every person in absolutely everything that they will undertake in the coming week. This should *not* be taken to imply that God's Spirit is not already operative in every place and situation that will be encountered. It does not require the believer's conscious awareness or physical presence for the Spirit of God to be operative.

The 'Come over to Macedonia!' model of mission (cf. Acts 16:9) is one helpful way of thinking about the dismissal. Of central importance is that the presence of God's Spirit does not depend upon the believer's conscious awareness or physical presence. God is at work already in any office, building site, call centre, seminar room, hospital ward, business meeting, in short, every particular workplace in which we might find ourselves. Even so, the dismissal or final blessing sends the congregation, with heightened sensitivities to the taste or aroma of the presence of God's Spirit, to share in God's activity in the world.

Worship leaders can help congregations to affirm the reality of heightened sensitivities to the taste or aroma of the presence of God's Spirit by various symbolic means. Mark Greene's pamphlet *Supporting Christians at Work* recounts how one church took the concept of being salt in the world from Matthew 5 and used it to create a brief but moving ceremony. Members of the congregation go forward and are given a small amount of salt in their hands. After a prayer of commitment to be salt in the world, they eat the few grains of salt as a sign of commitment and dedication to working as God's Spirit directs to break the curse of sin in workplaces around the globe.

Chapter 4

HUMAN RIGHTS IN THE WORKPLACE

'It took me twenty years to develop my temper,' said Michèle Le Doeuff when describing how she came slowly to confront the sexism of philosophy.[1] Learning to recognise that something was not right, and finding the language to speak its name, took time. Her journey from mutism to anger – from passive collaboration to 'fighting fire with fire', from silent acceptance to the articulation of new modes of accountability for the discipline – involved identifying the problem in everyday situations and conversations, and resisting the form of delegation which says: 'Go ahead, what you do costs me nothing.'[2] Le Doeuff found her anger and mobilised it for the sake of liberating 'the common-wealth' of philosophy from sexism. The process was, for her, a journey from the personal to the political. Her book *Hipparchia's Choice* can be read as the story of how Le Doeuff overcame anxieties that made it hard to confront the problem, kept her 'on the defensive' and inclined to keep her sadness to herself.[3]

This chapter is about learning to get angry in ways that befit the disciples of Christ Jesus about wages that are insufficient to sustain family life, unsafe and unhealthy working conditions, workplaces that tolerate bullying, and other injustices. Like Le Doeuff, Christian tradition has long recognised that anger can be a force for good. Paul writes: 'Be angry but do not sin; do not let the sun go down on your anger, and do not make room for the devil' (Ephesians 4:26–27). John Chrysostom teaches that anger has been implanted in the human soul by God so that evil may be chastised; Augustine that anger at a wrongdoer can seek his amendment.[4] Thomas Aquinas describes anger as a passion of Christ's soul and is convinced that anger is not always sinful: 'For Augustine says (on John 2:17) that "he is eaten up by zeal for the house of God, who seeks to better whatever he sees to be evil in it, and if he cannot right it, bears with it and sighs." Such was the anger that was in Christ.'[5] Major figures from Christian tradition repeatedly depict anger not only as a sin to be avoided but as the passion that should respond with discernment to the ungodly and that, when subjected to reason governed by love, moves the believer to appropriate action.

One of the most important questions in Christian ethics today is how to get angry in ways that befit the disciples of Christ Jesus. Aquinas comments as follows on Christ's anger at what the money-changers had done to the temple:

> For when sorrow is inflicted upon someone, there arises within him a desire of the sensitive appetite to repel this injury brought upon himself or others ... As to the desire of revenge it is sometimes with sin, i.e. when anyone seeks revenge beyond the order of reason: and in this way anger could not be in Christ, for this kind of anger is sinful. Sometimes, however, this desire is without sin – nay, is praiseworthy, e.g. when anyone seeks revenge according to justice, and this is zealous anger.[6]

Whereas sorrow accepts and succumbs to evil, anger attacks and endeavours to overcome it. Anger has a close relation to sorrow because it arises when an injury, slight, or such like, has caused one to feel sorrow. When imitative of Christ's anger, our anger is drawn toward something more excellent that heals the sorrow and corrects any wrongdoing. Mindful, however, that the passions, and anger especially, can be uncontrollable and capricious, Aquinas warns believers to be on their guard against these troubling aspects of anger.[7] Those things in response to which anger arises in a person belong to the external world which is constantly changing. Only Christ's anger was always in accordance with reason's *imperium* and ordered toward the justice of God.

The key point for Aquinas is that anger never disturbed Jesus' reason or obscured his judgements but was in complete synergy with his reason, grace and all the virtues.[8] '[O]f His own will', writes Aquinas, 'He subjected Himself to these corporeal and animal passions.'[9] Christ's full humanity includes being subject to the movement of the passions or what Aquinas calls the appetites of the sensitive soul that stand at the crossroads between body and soul.[10] Jesus' anger was blatant and public for all to see in the violent expulsion of the money-changers from the temple; he was 'consumed' with zeal for the Lord's house (Psalm 69:9; Matthew 21:12). Yet his passions inclined only to objects that were in total harmony with reason and thus ordered to God whereas the objects of the passions in all other humans tend also to objects that are not in conformity with reason and can be desired regardless of reason's command.[11]

The movement of Jesus' passions never preceded the judgement of reason, and their effects never impeded the use of reason. Hence his exemplary role for disciples seeking to integrate their passions into the moral life: 'Christ assumed our defects that He might satisfy for us, that He might prove the truth of His human nature, and that He might become an example of virtue to us.'[12] 'We have', says Aquinas, citing Hebrews 4:15, 'not a high-priest who cannot have compassion on our infirmities, but one tempted in all things like as we are, without sin.'[13] His focus on those passions that are the most disturbing and troubling for the human person emphasises not only that Christ's humanity cannot be abstracted from the passions but signifies that they participate fully in his perfection.

Every generation, implies Aquinas, is expected to ask why and how Christ's anger is exemplary. This means, perhaps, not allowing the limitations of our social and cultural world-views to tone down our anger to that which is socially and culturally acceptable. The claim in this chapter is that directing one's anger about the accursed nature of many workplaces means striving for the recognition of claim rights necessary for a decent standard of work and living, and for collective as well as individual claims. The claim is that present-day Christians must engage critically with cultural trends to prioritise civil and political rights over social, economic and cultural rights. This means not resting satisfied with liberty rights in the workplace but striving to protect not only the rights of individuals but also the legitimate claims of intermediate institutions, including trades unions.

JUSTICE AT WORK

'The UN proclaims, "Everyone has the right to rest and leisure, including reasonable limitation of working hours." I'll have my wife inform the baby.' So writes the politically right-wing humorist P. J. O'Rourke.[14] For our purposes, O'Rourke's satire points to difficult issues for many Christians. To what extent is modern rights-talk, including the language and conceptuality of human rights, tied up with modern notions of self-ownership, property rights, market exchange, and the unrestrained liberty of the individual? Can a Christian be faithful to biblical and traditional teaching and argue for a right to have rights? Is there a right to work? If so, of what kind? What about rights to decent working conditions and levels of pay?

I have written elsewhere about human rights in Christian perspective and argued that it is for Christ's sake, and the sake of his coming kingdom, that the rights of every person are to be recognised and respected; for his sake Christians affirm the human body has a claim to food and shelter.[15] *In Christ* believers know that natural life has been formed and given by God, and is to be preserved and protected for God's sake; bodily life contains within itself the right to its own preservation because God has willed the continuation of life. These are positive, not merely negative, rights that do more than protect against interference. Human rights legislation has a hidden kinship with Jesus' commandment to love to the extent that it militates against any victimisation of the disadvantaged.[16]

Others have made similar points. Witness Nicholas Wolterstorff's argument in *Justice: Rights and Wrongs*, that God is wronged by injustice and has the right to hold humans accountable for injustice. The wronging of a person is the source of rights because God's endowing of human beings with his image means that humans have worth. In Isaiah 1:17, Isaiah of Jerusalem says:

> Seek justice,
> rescue the oppressed,
> defend the orphan,
> plead for the widow.

Isaiah believes in God's salvation from poverty, alienation and oppression, and was not satisfied with contemplation. The poor are wronged by their destitution. So too are those left helpless and abandoned. The language might be modern but there is a recipient-side to the moral order: a recognition of the worth of human beings, and an indication that this worth grounds how a person should be treated. If these elements are present, it does not matter whether the language of rights is used; it is not the word that matters but the shape of the reasoning.

It must be recognised, of course, that the legislative human rights regime, as it has developed since World War 2, belongs to a particular historical era. It is deeply problematic in ways that need not be explored here. Many Christian thinkers have drawn attention to the potentially individualist and conflictual nature of rights discourse, its associations philosophically with private property, and tendency to foster a 'me, me, me' culture in societies where rights talk is highly developed.[17] Others have argued that Christians should recognise the non-necessary and contingent nature of rights-talk. In other words, it is not essential to Christian doctrine. Neither the Bible nor much of Christian tradition uses the language of subjective rights.

Yet, and this is the important point: the legislative human rights regime is a viable means of expressing the core Christian theological conviction that each and every human life is precious because loved by God. In the words of the American campaigning organisation, Evangelicals for Human Rights, all persons, regardless of ethnicity, sex, nationality, ability/disability, and social status,

> are to be perceived as sacred, as persons of equal and immeasurable worth and of inviolable dignity. Therefore they must be treated with the reverence and respect commensurate with this elevated moral status. This begins with a commitment to the preservation of their lives and protection of their basic rights.[18]

There is broad agreement in the Christian tradition regarding the material aims of the international human rights movement. So, for instance, the Orthodox scholar Vigen Guroian, who, as we shall see, rejects much modern rights theory, accepts

> that the deepest inspiration of the doctrine of human rights has roots in Christian convictions. God is person, and so are human beings, who are created in God's image and likeness. Every human *hypostasis* [personal existence–EDR] has needs and makes legitimate claims to certain advantages necessary for human flourishing.[19]

This is not the place to explore why, despite broad agreement with respect to material aims, some Christians believe modern rights thinking to be alien to Christianity whilst others hold the concepts of natural rights and inherent rights to be thoroughly biblical. We concentrate in what follows on rights-related questions in the workplace. Does it make good theological sense to speak of a right to work?

MORE THAN CIVIL AND POLITICAL RIGHTS REQUIRED

For some, it is harmful and nonsensical to speak of a right to work. 'Don't fall into the UN Declaration of Human Rights trap, where everyone is declared to have "the right to rest and leisure",' writes the satirist and social commentator P. J. O'Rourke.[20] 'Look where it's gotten the UN.' Focus instead on the trinity of basic principles identified by Adam Smith, the father of modern political economists: pursuit of self-interest, division of labour, and freedom of trade.[21] O'Rourke's summary of Adam Smith's *The Wealth of Nations* is marketed with the catchline: 'Now you don't have to read it. P.J. has done it for you.' And he certainly has a knack of getting to the heart of the matter provocatively. 'The whole business of authority', he says, 'is to interfere in other people's business. Princes and priests can never resist imposing restrictions on the pursuit of self-interest, division of labor, and freedom of trade.'[22] The phrase 'it's none of his business' should eventually upend 'everything that political and religious authorities have been doing for ten thousand years'.[23]

Is it, then, no one else's business – outside the employer/employee relationship – whether a person can get work and the standard of the wages afforded to workers? Do governments have obligations to create jobs for citizens? How are Christians to negotiate these questions?

P. J. O'Rourke serves for our purposes as a representative (albeit caricatured) of modern, neo-con liberalism, which preaches that there is nothing wrong with the pursuit of self-interest. More to the point, the purpose of laws is merely to ensure individual liberty. Writing laws should be nothing more than a way of furthering 'that natural liberty which it is the proper business of law, not to infringe, but to support'.[24] The ideal society is that in which every person is left perfectly free to pursue their own interest their own way, as long as they do not violate the laws of justice that provide for the protection of citizens. 'Mere justice is, upon most occasions, but a negative virtue, and only hinders us from hurting our neighbour.'[25]

In contrast to the commonplace modern, liberal assumption that the purpose of laws is to maximise individual liberty and facilitate the free movement of money, goods and services, Christians (and, indeed, members of all the Abrahamic faiths) are likely to prioritise human rights that provide for social justice – including protection for workers, decent wages, effective and equitable social welfare provision, and the like. Consider briefly the following texts. From the Tanakh (or Hebrew Bible):

> Justice, justice shall you pursue, that you may thrive and occupy the land which the LORD your God is giving you. (Deuteronomy 16:20 JSB)

> Announce to my people their rebellion … Look you serve your own interest on your fast day, and oppress all your workers. (Isaiah 58:1–3)

From the New Testament:

> When the Son of Man comes in his glory … All the nations will be gathered before him, and he will separate people one from another as a shepherd separates sheep from goats. (Matthew 25:31–32)

> Let the elders who rule well be considered worthy of double honour … for the scripture says, 'You shall not muzzle an ox while it is treading out the grain', and, 'The labourer deserves to be paid.' (1 Timothy 5:18)

From the Qur'an:

> O you who believe! do not devour your property among yourselves falsely, except that it be trading by your mutual consent; and do not kill your people; surely Allah is Merciful to you. (4:29)

> And We made your sleep to be rest (to you), And We made the night to be a covering, And We made the day for seeking livelihood. (78:9–11)

More texts could be cited. Biblical justification abounds as to why all Christian leaders should continue to voice clear and loud opposition to individualist claims that a strong theory of liberty-rights renders unnecessary the recognition of claim-rights in the workplace, and why collective rights are necessary in order to protect them. God heard the groaning of the Israelites in Egypt, on account of their taskmasters, and took action to deliver them (Exodus 2:24–25; Exodus 3:7–12). The law given to Moses entailed the provision that no labour was to be done on the Sabbath by manservant, maidservant, cattle, servant, or anyone (Exodus 20:9–10; Leviticus 23:28–36). Periods of collective rest were to be observed (Leviticus 23:36). Strict rules for the keeping of slaves were to be enforced (Exodus 21:1–4). Moses was to be relieved of some work when the burden became too heavy (Exodus 18:17–18). Ritual traditions of offering the first fruits of all labour to God presupposes that they have been acquired in manner pleasing to God (Exodus 23:16–19).

Suffice it for the moment to observe this point of agreement between the faiths – namely, that the struggle for social justice is broader than civil and political rights. By implication, a labour policy is good only when the objective rights of workers are respected.

LIBERTY-RIGHTS *AND* CLAIM-RIGHTS

Bridges must be built between theological and jurisprudential ways of thinking. To this end, we must be clear about what kinds of rights we are discussing. As a first step, it is useful to adopt Wesley N. Hohfeld's 1913 classification of rights into one of four kinds: liberty- or claim-rights, privilege- or immunity-rights. Hohfeld was an American jurist whose classification of rights encapsulated predominant streams of neo-Kantian thinking about rights and gained wide acceptance in the twentieth century because of its conceptual clarity. His classification was designed to be of use to two or more parties entering into a contract; each type of right has an associated correlate term that applies to the same relation when viewed from the perspective of the other agent.

A *claim-right* is that which one agent can demand from another because this right has a duty attaching to it. A claim right has an associated correlate term 'duty' that applies to the same relation when viewed from the perspective of the other agent, and is the most common kind of right. For example, if Mrs Anderson has employed John the window-cleaner at an agreed rate of pay, then John has a claim to be paid by Mrs Anderson. She, in turn, has a duty to pay John. Similarly, if a manufacturer of electronic goods sells a radio to a member of the public at an agreed price, that member of the public has a claim to that radio being of a proper standard of workmanship. This claim-right can be enforced at law (in the UK) through the Supply of Goods and Services Act 1982.

A *liberty-right* exists in the absence of a duty to refrain from a given act. For example, Mrs Anderson is at liberty to clean her own windows if that's what she wants to do. It would be up to her to decide; she has the freedom to do as she chooses. A liberty-right, says Hohfeld, has as its correlative a no-right – no other person has the right to stop her from doing what she wants to do. (In other words, the correlative of a 'claim-right' is another person's duty; the correlative of a 'liberty-right' is what Hohfeld calls a 'no-right'.) A liberty right is more like a kind of freedom than a right in the stricter sense of a claim-right.

A *privilege-right* is a kind of power. For example, Fred the tax inspector has the privilege or power to read John the window-cleaner's tax returns in the absence of any duty not to do so, that is, assuming he is not John's brother or otherwise involved personally with the case. Surgeons have the privilege or power to read a patient's medical notes prior to an operation. Correlative duties rest with the tax office and hospital to ensure appropriate data protection measures and management of the data.

An *immunity-right* is a kind of freedom from the power of another agent. For example, a diplomatic representative from another nation might be tax exempt for a period. Non-human animals could, in theory, be granted immunity-rights, for example freedom from cruel treatment during transportation. If granted, such immunity-rights could become a means of granting animals protection against individuals or corporations with respect to torture and cruelty. Correlative duties lie with the farmer or transport company to ensure that these immunity-rights are respected.

Hohfeld's categorisation requires us to ask whether the right to work is a liberty-right and/or a claim-right. As a liberty-right, the right to work is relatively uncontentious. Few would support the supposition that anyone should be excluded from the economic sphere and thus prevented from earning a living – though, of course, this was the case in apartheid societies. The International Covenant on Economic, Social and Cultural Rights (ICESCR) provides in article 6(1) for the 'right to work, which includes the right of everyone to the opportunity to gain his living by work'. When understood as a liberty-right, the right to work ensures that no one is excluded unfairly from the workplace on the grounds of sex, gender, skin-colour, ethnic background, class, or other such grounds. The state's correlative duty is to ensure that this right is protected.

The ICESCR also provides in article 6(2) that 'the full realization of this right shall include technical and vocational guidance and training programmes.' Article 1 of the European Social Charter states:

> With a view to ensuring the effective exercise of the right to work, the Contracting Parties undertake: …
> 3. to establish or maintain free employment services for all workers;
> 4. to provide or promote appropriate vocational guidance, training and rehabilitation.

These articles provide more than merely a liberty-right to work but require that member states provide opportunities for individuals to fulfil their potential to work. Not only are member states obligated not to destroy a person's opportunity to work by failing to protect against unfair discrimination, but they are also required to provide opportunities such that an individual can fulfil these opportunities. Hence member states are required to ensure that free employment services are available to all workers to avail them of opportunities of getting back into work in the event of unemployment, and also that 'appropriate vocational guidance, training and rehabilitation' is available.

European social legislation goes beyond a strict 'liberty' interpretation of the right to work. There are some 'claim' dimensions. Consider further:

- Article 23 of the UNDHR guarantees everyone 'the right to work, to free employment, to just and favourable conditions of work and to protection against unemployment'.

- Under article 1(2) of ILO Convention No. 122 each member shall ensure that 'there is work for all who are available for and seeking work'.
- Article 1 of the European Social Charter states:

> With a view to ensuring the effective exercise of the right to work, the Contracting Parties undertake:
> 1. to accept as one of their primary aims and responsibilities the achievement and maintenance of as high and stable a level of employment as possible, with a view to the attainment of full employment;
> 2. to protect effectively the right of the worker to earn his living in an occupation freely entered upon.

In these articles, the right to work asserts not only a liberty-right as it concerns non-discriminatory access to work but rights to standards of treatment in the workplace, stable economic conditions and employment policies oriented toward full employment. The requirements here are higher than merely the protection of a liberty-right to work. These claim-rights place correlative duties upon governments to ensure that the opportunity to *earn a living* means precisely that, that is, that wages are sufficient to enable a person (and their family) to live, and that the standard of that work is decent. (Privilege-rights and immunity-rights need not concern us here.)

CHRISTIAN ADVOCACY OF WORKPLACE RIGHTS

How, then, might Christian people position themselves in relation to these various rights claims? How strongly might Christian people want to support the kind of claim-rights specified above?

It is important to bear in mind at this point that, for some political theorists, support for claim-rights at work is risible. Forget 'high-minded screeds' that promise nonsense comparable with unalienable rights to steak, beer, rest, and leisure, writes P. J. O'Rourke.[26] Steak, beer, rest, and leisure! This is how O'Rourke dismisses the content of claim-rights at work. He is, of course, a humorist who is writing in large part to amuse. That said, the political edge to his writing is surely intentional. Once liberty-rights to work are secure, other rights are unnecessary if not harmful to the economy.

The only inalienable right that O'Rourke recognises is a liberty-right, or negative right, to freedom from interference. Provided that I remain within the law, no one may interfere with my liberty-right to participate in the production or service aspects of the economy and benefit from the profits accrued (or take the consequences if my business loses money). It is easy in the present-day political climate to accept O'Rourke's representation of familiar notions of rights as freedoms conceived in terms of individual autonomy and independence. 'There is only one basic human right, the right to do as you damn well please. And with it comes the only basic human duty, the duty to take the consequences.'[27]

In contrast, my claim is that Christian discipleship – that is, living in the knowledge that the resurrection broke the power of sin – properly entails campaigning and praying for (in whatever way we are capable) decent and humane work. This means more than support merely for the liberty-right to work. It means prioritising the struggle for protection for workers, a floor of employment rights that is both socially and economically beneficial, decent wages, macro-economic policies aimed at full employment, effective and equitable social welfare provision, legal measures to prevent monopolies and destructive competition that undercuts prices by compromising the well-being of workers, in ways consistent with biblically guided living for the sake of Christ and the coming kingdom of God on earth.

CORRECTING THE NEGLECT OF SOCIAL AND ECONOMIC RIGHTS

In our present-day social context, the question becomes how to construe the relationship between the two sets of rights recognised by the Universal Declaration of Human Rights: civil and political, on the one hand, and social, economic and cultural on the other.

Two International Covenants transform the UNDHR provisions into an international, normative regime: The International Covenant on Civil and Political Rights (ICCPR) and The International Covenant on Economic, Social and Cultural Rights (ICESCR). The official position of the United Nations Organisation is that the two Covenants and sets of rights are 'universal, indivisible and interdependent and interrelated; the international community must treat human rights globally in a fair and equal manner, on the same footing, and with the same emphasis.'

It is widely recognised that economic, social and cultural rights have often been neglected compared with their civil and political countparts.[28] Consider these recent rulings at the European Court of Human Rights (ECHR) and European Court of Justice (ECJ). I cite them as illustration of this tendency to prioritise civil and political claim-rights over economic, social and cultural claim-rights.

The first ruling was given by the ECHR in December 2008 to the effect that South Yorkshire Police should not have retained the DNA and fingerprints of two British men.[29] As reported by the BBC, the decision implied that keeping this information could not be regarded as necessary in a democratic society. The implications of the decision are likely to be far reaching. Under existing laws, the DNA profiles of everyone arrested for a recordable office in England, Wales and Northern Ireland have been kept on the database, regardless of whether they were charged or convicted. At the time of reporting, the details of 4.5 million people were said to be held, with one in five not having a criminal record.[30] The ECHR found that the police's actions were in violation of Article 8 of the European Convention on Human Rights and constituted a disproportionate interference with the applicants' right to respect for private life.

The ruling of the seventeen judges commented negatively on 'the blanket and indiscriminate nature of the power of retention in England and Wales' – the implication being that the UK government did not have this degree of leeway or 'margin of appreciation'. Jacqui Smith, the then Home Secretary, and senior police officers said they were disappointed with the ruling at the Strasbourg court, but human rights groups welcomed the unanimous judgement.[31] In other words, this ruling by the ECHR took a strong stance in favour of the civil and political claim-rights of the individuals whose data had been retained.

Less widely publicised but of equal concern are a succession of rulings by the ECJ concerning labour rights and the balance between the economic and social aims of the European Union over against the free movement provisions for the single market. The 'Legal Cases' pages of the European Trade Union Confederation (ETUC) website describes the cases as follows.

Briefly, the so-called Laval (or Vaxholm) case concerned whether Community law could restrict or prohibit trade unions in one Member State taking industrial action and whether the application of collective agreements in a host Member State can be restricted by Community law.[32] As reported by the ETUC, Swedish unions took action against a Latvian construction company Laval over the working conditions of Latvian workers refurbishing a school in the town of Vaxholm. Laval refused to sign a collective agreement, and a blockade of the workplace was initiated by the trade unions as a consequence. The Swedish Labour Court referred the case to the ECJ which ruled in December 2007 that the right to strike is a fundamental right, but not as fundamental as the right of businesses to supply cross-border services. The ETUC reaction was as follows: 'The ETUC position has always been for equality for migrant workers according to the conditions of the host country. The ruling amounts to a licence for social dumping, and key features of national industrial relations systems face being superseded by the free movement provisions.'[33]

In April 2008, the ECJ ruled in the Rüffert case that Member States may not adopt legislative measures which require contractors to pay wages that are in line with rates already agreed through collective bargaining agreements. In other words, contractors could pay workers brought into a site from another EU country less than existing workers whose pay rates were protected by a collective bargaining agreement. This case focused on whether public authorities have the right, when awarding contracts for work, to demand that tendering companies commit themselves to pay wages that are in line with rates already agreed through collective bargaining in the place where the work is done, or whether this amounts to a restriction on the freedom to provide services under Article 49 of the EC Treaty. The ruling represents a significant weakening of the economic rights of trade unions and workers.

As reported by the ETUC, the circumstances of the case were that the company Objekt und Bauregie GmbH & Co secured a contract for building work in Germany, which it subcontracted to a Polish firm, with an undertaking that it would ensure compliance with wage rates already in force on the site through collective agreement. The subcontract was withdrawn when it was discovered that the 53 posted workers were in fact earning 46.57% of the applicable minimum wage for the construction sector, and the Niedersachsen authority (a federal state in Lower Saxony, Germany) demanded costs. Dirk Rüffert, as the liquidator of the assets of Objekt and Bauregie, took legal action in a German national court to obtain payment of the penalty. The German national court referred the case to the ECJ. The ETUC condemned the subsequent ruling by the ECJ as destructive and damaging, amounting to an open invitation for social dumping, and warned that it could fuel public opposition to the internal market.

The ETUC also highlighted other cases, especially the so-called Viking and Luxembourg cases, as similarly negative for trade unions in the endeavour to remove obstacles to the free provision of cross-border services. Hence the ETUC's demand for a 'Social Progress Clause' to be linked to the Lisbon Treaty and for that Treaty and its fundamental freedoms 'to be interpreted as respecting workers' rights and collective action'.[34]

These cases are complex not only with respect to interpretations of the liberty-right to work but the content of claim-rights regarding wage levels in different parts of the EU, among other matters. The issues quickly become embroiled in regional protectionism, national loyalties and even racism. Specialist labour lawyers, trades unionists, policy-framers and others are needed to work on the details. In broad terms, however, my claim is that Christian people should not grant an elevated or preferred status to civil liberties and political freedoms as compared to social, economic and cultural rights, that is, that there is a symbiotic relationship between these concerns – the practical implication being that human rights in Christian perspective require that social, economic and cultural rights enjoy constitutional and legal parity with civil and political rights. They illustrate both how difficult, and how vitally important, it is that Christian people resist the drift toward human rights becoming mere symbols to protect the 'liberal icon' of private property.

These cases also warn against over-reliance on EU legislation and the incorporation of the European Convention on Human Rights (ECHR) into UK law to ensure protection for workers. Article 11 of the ECHR gives a right to peaceful assembly and to freedom of association with others, including the right of the individual 'to form and to join trade unions for the protection of his interests'. As illustrated above, case law from the Strasbourg institutions is failing to deliver meaningful protection for trade union activities. Lord Wedderburn asked in 2000: 'Will the new positive rights for individual workers be effective and sufficient protections without substantial collective combination?'[35] He spoke of unions being required to genuflect 'at the altar of individualism' in matters relating to training and grievances.[36] And his words seem to be coming true. A strong guarantee of fundamental individual rights is not sufficient condition for the protection of individuals, whether alone or in groups.

FRAMING LAW FOR THE COMMON GOOD

In 1996, just prior to a general election, the Roman Catholic Bishops of England and Wales wrote in a document entitled *The Common Good*:

> There can be a substantial imbalance of economic power between an isolated individual employee and a large

employer, and this imbalance is not corrected merely by the fact that the employee has entered into a contract. Contracts between unequal parties are a potent source of structural injustice.[37]

The Common Good opened with (to my mind) inspirational paragraphs about why religion is always personal but never just a private affair, why the deepening of the spiritual life must go hand in hand with social action, how the Church has both the right and the duty to advocate a social order in which the human dignity of all is fostered and to protest when it is in any way threatened. The bishops were clear that the Church does not present a political programme, but they drew on the corpus of Roman Catholic social teaching to affirm the Church's mission to restore in contemporary society the priority of the human over the economic, and the priority of the spiritual and moral over the material. The document held fast to these principles:

- the dignity of the human person;
- solidarity with our neighbour;
- faith has a social dimension;
- sin can find expression in the structures of society;
- subsidiarity;
  - the human race is a 'community of communities';
- solidarity;
  - evangelisation means bringing the Gospel into every stratum of human existence.

The Common Good urged Christian citizens in modern Britain not only to accord due respect to those who exercise legitimate political authority but to vote in ways that they believed would contribute to the good of society, be in the interests of justice and in pursuit of the 'option for the poor'. Regarding work, the bishops were clear that work is about more than making a living: it can and should be a participation in God's creative activity. Nor are workers mere commodities to be bought and sold: they have rights which are superior to the rights of capital and are entitled to a fair share of rewards that result from increased profits.

Today, the need to frame law for the common good is as great as ever. So too is the need for intermediate organisations: trades unions, the bishops argued, have a role in correcting the imbalance between employer and employee (§ 96) and manifest the principles of solidarity and the right of association – both of which are compatible if not necessary to a Christian understanding of the common good. Society's common good requires the legal protection of collective identities and bargaining arrangements. Hence Catholics should join an appropriate trade union, where possible. Employers are not entitled to negate the right of workers to join a trade union and have a duty to pay a just wage.

Unions have a correlate duty to conduct their affairs in accordance with the common good. Significantly, however, *The Common Good* states that society's common good is likely to require the legal protection of collective identities and bargaining arrangements.[38] The bishops are clear that Christians should be concerned about – and, indeed, accord some priority to – employment standards, protection of the right to work, full-employment policies, and other measures for the benefit of workers, especially the low paid.

The bishops' teaching is sourced, in large part, by Aquinas's teaching with respect to the common good. Aquinas favours the good of 'the whole' over the good of 'the part' or 'the one only', and orders all these goods toward God the supreme or highest good:

> the good of one becomes common to many, if it flows from the one to the other: and this can only be when the one, by its own action, communicates it to the others: and if it has not the power to transmit it to others, that good remains its own property. Accordingly, God communicated His goodness to His creatures in such wise that one thing can communicate to another the good it has received. Therefore it is derogatory to the divine goodness to deny things their proper operations.[39]

God, who is the supreme good – the *Summum Bonum* – from whom all other goods are derived, is the ultimate end of the entire universe. All goods are related to the *Summum Bonum* who is above and anterior to them all, holding all within a cosmic, metaphysical and ontological unity of divine purpose.[40] The common good is greater than the good of one only because it more perfectly reflects the oneness and order of the divine plan; it is closer to God's own unity in relation.

In a spirit of ecumenical sharing, it is surely possible for all Christians to argue that law should be framed for the benefit of the common good; the whole is always better than its parts because it reflects more perfectly the good of creation within the will of God. Social and economic goods should not be reduced to the aggregate of their worth to individuals. Nor should collective rights be recognised only as a subversive political move to ensure that individual rights are protected. Prioritising the common good need not threaten individual rights in ways that some liberals fear. To the contrary, it must belong to the perfection of creation that we share a common good. The disciples of Christ must surely protest at working practices that lead away from this goal.

Chapter 5

LOST VOCATIONS

While writing this chapter, two novels by J. G. Ballard were never far from my mind.

Cocaine Nights (1996) is about retired British and French expatriates in the Spanish coastal resort of Estrella de Mar. They belong to a seemingly idyllic community, enjoying a lifestyle of constant cultural and sporting activity – based around the thriving Club Nautico. *Cocaine Nights* is a detective novel with a dark side. Beneath the civilised surface of this world without work lie secret operations of crime, drugs and illicit sex, orchestrated by a charismatic Pied Piper figure named Crawford, whose dark influence is spreading with alarming speed.[1] 'Our governments', says Crawford, 'are preparing for future without work':

> Leisure societies lie ahead of us, like those you see on this coast. People will still work – or, rather, some people will work, but only for a decade of their lives. They will retire in their late thirties, with fifty years of idleness in front of them. A billion balconies facing the sun …[2]

Estrella de Mar is a leisure society in which politics fails to excite and religion demands 'a vast effort of imaginative and emotional commitment, difficult to muster if you're still groggy from last night's sleeping pill'.[3] The only force that rouses this tranquil (or is it tranquillised?) community is crime. Only burglaries, beatings, illicit sex, fraud, and more besides, quicken the nervous system and stir this bored community back to life.

The novel *Super-Cannes* (2000) is also about 'keeping the juices flowing' by tapping into the darker strains in human nature in advanced capitalist societies.[4] Like *Cocaine Nights*, its setting is a paradise in the new Riviera but for work-obsessed, top-drawer professionals, not the leisured classes. Eden-Olympia is a business park like no other. All of the most powerful multinationals have offices in this complex where leisure has been replaced by a grudging corporate puritanism in which work yields all the fulfilment an individual needs and the primary objective is to turn money into money: 'At Eden-Olympia work is the ultimate play, and play the ultimate work.'[5]

The traditional moral compass-bearings of the Church, family and even the law have fallen away to be replaced by whatever morality is chosen by the successful. Eden-Olympia's air-conditioned business park is a vast complex devoid of (among other things) children, cultural and community life, town councils, magistrates' courts and citizens' advice bureaux: 'representative democracy ... [is] replaced by the surveillance camera and the private police force.'[6] As in Friedrich Nietzsche's *On the Genealogy of Morals,* the very meaning of good and evil is cut free from religion and culture to be defined by a powerful elite. Yet these societies have problems.

Despite the high-tech standards of hygiene at Eden-Olympia, the new race of work-addicted people tend to get sick. Energy levels begin to fall after twelve months. CEOs without human ties but with enormous power have trouble sleeping, complain about the quality of air, worry about health hazards, develop respiratory complaints, inexplicable headaches and pains, and so on. As in *Cocaine Nights*, the chilling 'solution' is crime. The anti-hero of *Super-Cannes* finds that violence produces the desired effect. 'I'm talking', says Wilder Penrose the resident psychologist, 'about a carefully metered violence, microdoses of madness like the minute traces of strychnine in a nerve tonic.'[7] Violence is therapeutic.

One young executive happened upon a woman tourist being mugged and went to her rescue.

> 'While she called the police he gave the fellow a good beating, kicked him so hard that he broke two bones in his

> right foot. He came in a week later to have the cast removed, and I [i.e., Penrose] asked him about the dermatitis. It had gone. He felt buoyant and confident again. Not a trace of depression.'[8]

Ballard does not shrink from his subject matter and violence is prescribed at Eden-Olympia as a most potent cure.[9] While his block-buster 'who-dunnits'/'why-dunnits' are rarely rated by critics as of the highest literary standard, they probe some of our deepest collective pathologies. 'The main reason for reading Ballard nowadays', writes Stephen Moss, 'is the truth one finds in his fiction – truth that one can see reflected in any day's news stories.'[10]

'WILLING SLAVES'?

Eden-Olympia represents an extreme and is a long way from many of our workplaces. Ballard's truth is like that of science fiction in which authors imagine a future and display the repercussions of certain types of behaviour by central characters. Yet the novels reflect issues that arise in real workplaces. If Ballard is right, as I think he is, the relation between work and leisure in present-day Western societies is often beset by problems. Either we work in order to acquire leisure but then neglect to make this leisure worthwhile, or the pressures of work are such that time for quality leisure is squeezed out. *Either way, it is hard to hold onto a sense of work as vocation.*

Madeleine Bunting's study of overwork and despair in British workplaces today raises similar concerns.[11] She analyses the impact on individuals and families of employers 'wanting blood' to the extent that home life is damaged, workplaces have rising incidences of depression, company loyalty counts for little, and the threat of redundancy is commonplace. Bunting describes workplaces in which people are so absorbed by what they do that there is no start, and no end, to what they are doing. Citing an ex-employee who describes how, during her period of employment, the company and its aims were the whole of her life, she writes: 'There's a lot of people here who get into trouble. They are addicted to Microsoft.

They're in denial, but they live, eat and breathe Microsoft. It's their world.'[12] This kind of workplace is one in which there is tremendous pressure to perform 'at the bleeding edge of technology'.[13] To stay ahead of the competition requires the submission of all human needs to the company's requirements.

For many people today, work is rewarding and enjoyable. It pays the bills and is integral to our sense of personal identity, social identity, and role in society. For the very fortunate few, work does all this *and* carries a sense of vocation. These lucky people derive from work not only affluence but also a sense of dignity and privilege in serving others – for example, as a teacher in the classroom, a policeman or -woman keeping our streets safe, a prison officer helping to rehabilitate inmates, a dental technician obsessed about the cleanliness of his or her equipment, a business-person creating jobs for others. Yet this is not true for everyone. Many factors in present-day workplaces conspire to make it increasingly difficult for employees to experience their work as vocational.

At the higher end of the income scale, the concept of vocation does not sit easily with working practices more fiercely competitive than anything described by Darwin in *The Origin of Species*. When individual employees are deemed to be as good only as the financial merits of the next contract they secure, the concept of vocation can easily be choked by anxiety and the need to be seen to perform. As recent TUC campaigns about working time have highlighted, systems of internal competition amongst staff often result in staff working considerable amounts of unpaid overtime with knock-on consequences for work–life balance and family commitments.[14] Constant threats of 'downsizing' and failure to safeguard pensions impact heavily on family life and civic society.

People have less and less time to volunteer for good causes or act as councillors. Nine out of ten people wanted to spend less time at work and more time with family and friends, a recent survey revealed.[15] Poor management practices can contribute to high levels of anxiety that tend to corrode an ethos of service and commitment to the common good. The negative implications for a sense of vocation of some managerial techniques – for example, superficial commitment to the autonomy of the worker in return for total devotion to the brand, increasingly subtle methods of controlling employee behaviour, the bureaucratisation of ethics and moral reasoning – are all enormous.

Lower down the income scale, employees are also often under pressure to work longer and more intensively. The TUC's recent report on agency workers in the UK states that as many as 20 per cent of the UK workforce are at risk of exploitation because of their employment status, ignorance of their rights, or lack of information in their own language; agency staff are paid 80p for every pound paid to permanent staff doing a similar level of job; agency staff in post for more than a year do not gain the enhanced employment rights other workers would enjoy after 12 months in a job as they normally do not have the legal rights of an employee, and more besides.[16] Those with relatively low-level skills are affected especially. A recent report by the Joseph Rowntree Foundation studied the geography of employment in Great Britain and found large spatial concentrations of worklessness. Low skills can have a sapping effect on self-esteem, it reports. 'Those who have a negative experience of education at school are less likely than average to engage in learning in adulthood.'[17]

In geographical areas of the country identified by the Social Exclusion Unit in 2004 as 'concentrations of worklessness', over half of the working-age population has no qualifications. Considerable effort needs to be invested, the report concludes, not only in helping individuals to access a first job but also to move on to more satisfactory jobs.[18] Older workers with low skills, little pension provision and health issues find labour market participation especially difficult. Many people who have had disadvantaged working lives, argues another Rowntree Foundation report, find it difficult to sustain work up until state pension age.[19] In this context, a theological exploration of vocation seems like a middle-class luxury.

HYPOCRISY, DELUSION AND LACK OF CERTAINTY

Further problems beset a theology of vocation. Hypocrisy in the lives of church members is still widely cited as a reason why secularist humanists, and others, choose to place faith elsewhere than in the one, true God. It is always possible, moreover, that Christian people delude themselves with notions of false vocations. The Rodgers and Hammerstein musical *The Sound of Music* enjoyed a revival recently in London's West End. Live audiences, once again, enjoyed the nuns gossiping about Maria who climbed trees, waltzed on her way to mass, had curlers in her hair, and was late for everything except for every meal. My memories of the musical are of the 1965 film in which the Reverend Mother, played by Peggy Wood, wonders if Maria's vocation might lie outside the convent: 'It seems to be the will of God that you leave us … only for a while, Maria … Perhaps if you go out into the world for a time, knowing what we expect of you, you will have a chance to find out if you can expect it of yourself.' Her words were spoken wisely. Maria thought that her vocation was the high calling of the convent. As it played out, she was to be a wife and stepmother.

Jesus' warning is that some who think they are prophesying and doing mighty deeds in the Lord's name will be told on the last day that they have deluded themselves:

> 'Not everyone who says to me, "Lord, Lord", will enter the kingdom of heaven, but only one who does the will of my Father in heaven. On that day many will say to me, "Lord, Lord, did we not prophesy in your name, and cast out demons in your name, and do many deeds of power in your name?" Then I will declare to them, "I never knew you; go away from me, you evildoers." ' (Matthew 7:22–23)

These frightening words suggest that there are false vocations and that we shall not know definitively until the day of judgement whether we have understood our vocation aright. Even if believers have acted in Jesus' name to prophesy and cast out demons, that is, those things that Jesus instructed his apostles to do, they might not have been doing the will of God. Outward acts of prophesying, giving talks, and so on, can be done unjustly, covetously, unmercifully and without love.

Nor can believers be certain that their vocation – or what they believe to be their vocation – is such in the eyes of God. The Gospel of Mark records Jesus' words: 'Eloi, Eloi, lama sabachthani?' which means, 'My God, my God, why have you forsaken me?' (Mark 15:34). Jesus' words echo the desolation and bewilderment of Psalm 22. His earlier sense of being sent by the Father (John 20:21) appears to be wavering and is replaced with such a depth and intensity of suffering that he cries aloud. His anguish is evident. In full solidarity with subsequent generations of disciples who have no assurance of their vocation but, rather, feel abandoned and overlooked by God, Jesus underwent the tragic experience of complete desolation. 'Jesus' human soul was reduced to a wasteland.'[20]

Jesus had put himself into the hands of God utterly. Even so, his words from the cross suggest anguish and exhaustion rather than certainty of vocation. Is it, then, likely that his disciples will be guaranteed an easier way of life? Surely not. Believers might want a sense of vocation and the assurance that they are fulfilling God's purpose for their lives. But it is not a guaranteed benefit of discipleship. If we want a sense of vocation because it makes us feel good, says the Orthodox priest Thomas Hopko, this is less than perfect love. If we want to find fulfilment as a person, that is wonderful and desirable. Of itself, however, it is not spiritual perfection.[21] Rather, if our prayer is patterned after Christ, then we may expect to feel forsaken by God and to know darkness of the soul. Our only assurance is that Christ Jesus has compassion on our weakness because he shared our humanity. He was 'in all points tempted as we are, yet without sin' (Hebrews 4:15).

SO WHAT? ABANDON THE NOTION OF 'VOCATION'?

Should Christian people, then, abandon talk of vocation? Is this word and its associated conceptuality so beset by problems that we should devote our energies elsewhere? In Chapter 1, we alluded to the many instances in Christian history when the language of vocation put a spiritual gloss on work that is underpaid, degrading, unsafe and exploitative. These are serious charges. The language of vocation is both difficult to revive against the backdrop of this history and often unhelpful in its association with an unattainable ideal. Should we abandon it?

No! Even the most cursory glance at the New Testament reveals many instances in which Jesus called (Greek *kaleō*) ordinary people to be his disciples (Matthew 4:21; Mark 6:7) and called sinners to repentance and the people to himself (Matthew 9:13; Mark 8:34; Luke 9:1); many instances in which disciples were called (*proskaleō*) to build up the Church and preach the gospel (Acts 13:2; Acts 16:10); and many more in which Paul speaks of his own intense sense of being called (*klētos*, Romans 1:1), of others being 'called of Christ' (Romans 1:6, 8:30, 9:11, 25; 1 Corinthians 7:18–24; Ephesians 4:1–4; Philippians 3:14; 1 Thessalonians 2:12; 2 Thessalonians 1:11; 1 Peter 3:9) for the sake of the gospel, and, indeed, of all things being called to work together according to the divine purpose (Romans 8:28).

So many instances of calls to embrace the work of God pervade the New Testament that we cannot simply abandon either the language of 'vocation' or the importance of a sense of call in the lives of some believers. Yet we have to face the problems outlined above with respect to the language of 'vocation' and 'call' and ask what is needed to correct them. Is the problem that we expect too little of God's grace? Or are there problems at the heart of how we think about vocation? My contention is that, yes, there is something wrong with much modern theological talk about vocation.

We tend to think about vocation in the terms set by our modern/postmodern context in terms of the relationship between an individual and their work or the relationship between an individual and God with respect to their work. Academic theology tends to reinforce this tendency and repeat the problem – even when trying to correct it.

This might not sound like a problem. My contention, however, is that it risks misrepresenting the relationship between God and humanity primarily in terms of individuals rather than primarily in terms of a people or community – God's chosen people of Israel, the other peoples of the earth, and the New Testament community of the body of Christ. This is not to downplay the role of persons as individuals in the divine plan. It is, however, to attempt to spell out the notion of vocation and/or call in biblical rather than modern, individualist terms.

This is the crux of the matter. Biblical accounts of the relationship between God and humanity do not tend to be conceived primarily in terms of relationships between individuals but between the Triune God and the whole of creation, involving peoples, communities and other groupings. Relationships between God and individual persons belong, secondarily, in this context of the primacy of the people. The challenge is to reflect this in how we think about vocation.

The Dutch theologian Marcel Sarot made this point recently. He drew attention to the three New Testament accounts of Saul's conversion (Acts 9:4, 22:7, 26:14). In all these accounts, Jesus asks Saul, 'Why do you persecute me?' The implication is that, by persecuting his followers, Saul was persecuting Jesus himself. Jesus identified himself with his body the Church. 'By becoming a Christian, one becomes part of the Christian community, and since this community is Christ, one thereby becomes part of the relationship between Father and the Son'.[22] This raises questions about the nature of this relationship between Christ and the Church as a relationship of *participation by grace not nature* that we cannot pursue here. Instead, we test the thesis about the primacy of the community or people over the individual in a Christian theology of vocation by looking in more detail at the life and teaching of the apostle Paul.

VOCATION NOT PRIMARILY AN INDIVIDUAL EXPERIENCE

The apostle Paul had a very clear sense of personal vocation. Many texts suggest that he saw himself as a man appointed to a particular role and set of responsibilities: a servant of Jesus Christ, called to be an apostle (Romans 1:1; 1 Corinthians 1:1; Galatians 1:11). The intensity of his call was clear:

> when God, who had set me apart before I was born and called me through his grace, was pleased to reveal his Son to me … I did not confer with any human being … (Galatians 1:15)

His prophet-like awareness of being called by God imbues his ministry with confidence and a sense of urgency. In contrast to Jesus' apparent loss of certainty with respect to his sense of vocation, Paul's words burst with conviction. His prayer is not for certainty – he has that already – but that his work might not be in vain (Phililippians 2:16; 1 Thessalonians 2:1; 1 Thessalonians 3:5).

Significantly, Paul understands his personal vocation only in relation to God's wider purposes for salvation. His strong statement of personal apostleship in Romans 1:1 is linked to the calling of the Christians in Rome to belong to Jesus Christ (Romans 1:6) and to their calling to sainthood (Romans 1:7). His vision of the growth of the Church is based on his belief that God is working together with those called 'according to his purpose' (Romans 8:28 NKJV). For Paul, vocation is not primarily an individual experience but has meaning only against the backdrop of the vocation of the Church. *The vocation of the Church has primacy over God's calling of individuals.* The whole Church shares the calling to live as the body of Christ and preach his name amongst Jew and gentile alike. Only in the context of the calling of Christian community as the body of Christ to proclaim the gospel does Paul speak of his personal calling as an apostle. The single-mindedness of Paul's sense of personal vocation is grounded in his conviction that the Church lives in a different (eschatological) order from the fleshly modes of existence that do not acknowledge Christ's Lordship, and because God has called the whole Church to the hope of glory to come.

Paul's experience and teaching offer a corrective to some familiar, present-day notions of vocation in Christian communities today. Too often we think of vocation as something that belongs or is given primarily to an individual. Paul realigns our thinking by reminding us that, for disciples of Christ, a personal vocation has no meaning apart from the divine purpose made known in Christ that both Jew and gentile should know the fellowship of the Son, Jesus Christ our Lord (1 Corinthians 1:9). Too often the question asked in pastoral settings today is: 'What is God calling you to do?' The question is not wrong. My point here is not that church leaders, priests and pastors stop asking it of those in their spiritual care. In 1 Corinthians 12:12–26 Paul affirms that every person is different and has his or her own distinctive role to play. Paul's corrective to our highly individualised culture, however, urges us to ensure that questions about personal calling are not divorced from the broader vocation of the Church. In our culture of privatised religion, the temptation is that we view personal vocations as given to individuals rather than part of God's action in the world through Christ's body the Church.

It is fashionable in some American churches these days to hold 'vocation Sundays' that focus on God's guidance in the lives of individuals. A large charitable organisation called the Lilly Endowment Inc. launched a programme for the Theological Exploration of Vocation in 1999.[23] Since then, many ministers, teachers in seminaries, university lecturers and others have been helped in their encouragement of young and old alike as they seek God's guidance for their lives. The programme focuses on the identification and nurture of leadership potential whether in congregations, business or professional organisations. And this is surely wonderful. Members of church communities are encouraged to feel a clear and strong sense of divine guidance. It is a blessing to sing George Herbert's poem 'The Call' – which speaks directly to questions of vocation and is a familiar choice – on Vocations Sunday:[24]

> Come, my Way, my Truth, my Life:
> Such a Way as gives us breath:
> Such a Truth as ends all strife:
> Such a Life as killeth death.
>
> ...
>
> Come, my Joy, my Love, my Heart:
> Such a Joy, as none can move:
> Such a Love, as none can part:
> Such a Heart, as joys in love.

Again, however, Paul's experience and teaching makes us pause and rethink. His teaching, I suggest, is that vocations are not given primarily to individuals but to the Church. Personal vocations belong within the eschatological, cosmic calling of the Church, giving us a different perspective on the matter. Every believer as a member of the Church *always has a vocation* by virtue of their membership of Christ's body. Moreover, Paul's everyday work to earn a living is *not* conceived by him as a divine vocation.

VOCATION NOT A MIDDLE-CLASS PRIVILEGE

Vocation is not necessarily something that must be sought in the workplace. When delimited in this way, a sense of vocation rapidly becomes the domain of the middle classes. Nothing in biblical teaching suggests that vocation is a middle-class privilege. Acts 18:3 records Paul as being a tentmaker or person who makes travel goods (the Greek adjective is *skēnopoios*). The text suggests that he worked day by day to earn his living and argued the truth of the gospel every Sabbath. In Corinthians 9:12 he draws attention to the fact that he does not accept financial support for his preaching of the gospel – because, we assume, he insists on working for a living as he travels. He would rather endure anything than 'put an obstacle in the way of the gospel of Christ' (1 Corinthians 9:12). Earning a living is part of Paul's vocation as an apostle only in so far as it gives him financial independence. His work as a tentmaker appears to be understood by him as relating *indirectly*, not directly, to his vocation as an apostle.

Paul's clear distinction between day-to-day work to earn a living and his vocation as apostle warns against notions of vocation that reinforce middle-class privilege. Instead, he understands his vocation in eschatological terms. 'A confidence like Paul's that one's work can have meaning in the context of the divine purpose, cannot exist in any real sense apart from some understanding of what the divine purpose is.'[25] In light of the hope of Christ's return and its inauguration of a new era, the everyday business of making a living is relatively insignificant. Nor does Paul focus especially on how his tentmaking mediates the will of God in his life. He does not allude to his particular craftmanship and skill as evidencing a divine calling to work with his hands. The assumption, rather, is that this workaday part of his life is subsumed within the command to love one's neighbour as oneself (Romans 13:9–10, 15:2; Galatians 5:14).

As a rabbi, Paul would have assumed that physical and other labour was part of daily, obedient living before God. As a Christian, he does not attempt to overturn this norm or the routines of daily existence but expects that believers will bear witness to Christ within the accepted patterns of their lives. Paul expects believers to support themselves wherever possible; 'for we intend to do what is right not only in the Lord's sight but also in the sight of others' (2 Corinthians 8:21; cf. 1 Thessalonians 4:11–12). Despite the hope of Christ's imminent return, the ordinary requirements of daily life still apply to the believer. Wage-earners are to remain wage-earners. Deacons responsible for ensuring the daily distribution of food to widows and other non-wage-earners are to conduct themselves honourably (1 Timothy 12:3–4). In other words, the normality of daily life is taken for granted by Paul and is *not* elevated by him with to the level of a vocation or particular call.

Paul's correctives run in stark contrast to many of the influences in workplaces today. Consider *Leading with Soul* by Terry Deal and Lee Bolman, a supposedly ground-breaking book which tells the story of their search for the true meaning of leadership in business. 'More and more,' the authors say, 'individuals are pondering a question posed by Jesus two thousand years ago: what does it profit us if we gain the world but lose our souls?'[26] Step One of their 'solution' is to recognise that signs of spiritual hunger and restlessness are everywhere, not least amongst young dot-com millionaires and entrepreneurs who have lost touch with what is really important in life. Step Two is to urge that today's business leaders bring together concepts from religion, spirituality, psychotherapy, philosophy, and more besides, if their companies are to liberate the latent energy in employees for more productive use.

Terry Deal and Lee Bolman offer a secularised account of vocation that binds spirituality and executive leadership together, thereby increasing the passion and sense of purpose that employees might find at work. Their book is an extreme example of a particular genre. They are not alone, however, in conceiving of work as a new spirituality of self-realisation. The Ballard novels cited earlier point in this direction too. No longer is formal employment (probably highly paid) in sharp contrast to leisure or play, religion or spirituality, because work subsumes both in a set of ends (personal and corporate) that saturate the life of the individual. Work has become 'a performance of the whole individual' characterised by an intensity that overshadows other activities and can appear to fulfil personal needs for socialisation and achievement, identity and even spirituality.[27] The notion of 'vocation' can feed into and support this world-view. Deal and Bolman's book is an extreme example. Yet the ideas they purport take milder form in many workplaces. The notion of 'vocation' can easily become a quasi-spiritual guise for a fiercely competitive workplace ethic.

VOCATION NOT RESERVED FOR THE CLERGY OR CHURCH LIFE

Does this mean that vocations are only for the clergy? Or for Christians in their church-related lives exclusively? The argument above is that Christian discipleship does not necessarily place a theological or spiritual obligation on believers to seek their vocation in the workplace. Some might feel their jobs to be 'the task Thy wisdom has assigned', to borrow Charles Wesley's words. Others might not. Does this mean, then, that only the ordained really have vocations?

No! Those ordained to ministry within the Church have hugely important callings but they are not the only people with vocations. We must not slip into an either/or scenario. It is not the case that *either* the only real vocations are apostolic or ordained *or* that every Christian must seek their vocation in the workplace. Rather, with Paul, the Church is the context within which to make sense of a personal sense of vocation. 'To Paul there is only one calling, the service of Christ.'[28] No aspect of life falls outside the Lordship of

Christ. He did not divide his life into 'sacred' versus 'secular'; his was not a 'two-spheres' theology of the kind that separates the holy and supernatural from the worldly, profane and natural. To the contrary. Every aspect of life is viewed by Paul in light of the eschatological hope. Every Christian's vocation is to direct themselves toward this hope and live for God's sake.

Vocations are not reserved only for the clergy. 'I beg you', says Paul to every member of the congregation, 'to lead a life worthy of the calling to which you have been called, with all humility and gentleness, with patience, bearing with one another in love …' (Ephesians 1:1–4). The calling to live in the Spirit and in 'the hope of your calling' belongs to all. Neither, however, is the effect of Paul's teaching to keep talk about vocation out of the workplace. Beware an either/or way of thinking. It is not a question of, on the one hand, a great many Christians with workplace vocations versus, on the other, a 'two-sphere' mode of thinking that confines vocation to the sacred or ecclesial aspects of life.

Equally, there is no need to restrict Christian talk about vocation to the personal vocations of individuals lucky enough to have a sense of calling with respect to how they earn a living. Nor need the language of vocation be delimited exclusively to the calling of the Church as an entire community or body – as if its life could be kept distinct from the day-to-day work of its members. In the next chapter, we try to avoid these pitfalls and think further about how every Christian's work (understood broadly as activity or effort expended towards an end so as to include all the above) is drawn into the Church's calling to serve Christ.

Chapter 6

WILL THERE BE WORK IN HEAVEN?

'A common observation is that the things people seem to enjoy most (e.g. food, drink, sex) are not envisioned as part of Heaven. I guess we shouldn't expect wifi or good mobile phone coverage there either.' So writes the journalist Tim Finin in an article entitled: 'Will your Blackberry work in heaven?'[1] The question: 'Will there be work in heaven?' is odd in many respects — like asking whether there be yodelling or jacuzzis! To the extent that heaven is not the kind of place, or state of being, that we might visit to verify or falsify answers, the question is bunkum or humbug; comparable to questions that have no meaning such as: 'What's the sound of one hand clapping?' or 'What's the square root of Saturday?' It would be as profitable to recite verses from Lewis Carroll's poem Jabberwocky as to pursue the question 'Will there be work in heaven?'

> 'Twas brillig, and the slithy toves
> Did gyre and gimble in the wabe:
> All mimsy were the borogoves,
> And the mome raths outgrabe.

The poem is an in-joke for those familiar with the meanings that Carroll attaches to the nonsense words. Readers with a taste for the 'deeply meaningful' who seek layers of signification are likely to be ridiculed.

So too, we might suppose, with questions about heaven. They are nonsensical! In pursuing such questions, we'd become like Alice in *Through the Looking Glass* when she commented on the Jabberwocky: 'Somehow it seems to fill my head with ideas – only I don't exactly know what they are!'

'Will there be work in heaven?' Is this question really nonsensical? Does it fill our heads with vague and fanciful ideas? Or is it precisely the kind of question required to help us explicate the connections between work and core Christian beliefs? I argue in this chapter that the question is *not* nonsensical. To the contrary, the central claim is that the hope of heaven informs an ethic of work in ways that help us to describe the relationship between the gospel of Christ and human work. This claim has three parts:

1. *The hope of heaven remains an inspiration to believers in their work.* Despite the relative dearth today of theological reflection on heaven and hell as they concern Christian ethics, personal identity after death, and such like, the hope of heaven remains important in the spiritual life.
2. *The hope of heaven gives eternal significance to earthly work.* In Christ, and because of the resurrection, human actions acquire an eternal dimension. Everything we do in the workplace matters because nothing included in Christ's resurrection will be lost.
3. *Guidance for an ethic of work can be derived from Jesus' words: 'as in heaven, so on earth'.* The Christian hope, learned from Jesus' words in the Lord's Prayer, is that heavenly work and the fulfilling of God's will is synonymous with love: work as love, and love as work. This conviction can provide the core of a Christian ethic of work.

WHATEVER HAPPENED TO THE HOPE OF HEAVEN?

A Warp cartoon on my desk shows St Peter waving a chequered flag as a weary runner enters the gates of heaven. I cannot remember the last sermon that I heard preached on the hope of heaven. Yet this cartoon has inspired me to keep going on more than one occasion!

That few sermons these days are preached on the hope of heaven may be explained, perhaps, by the relative dearth of recent (Protestant) theological reflection on heaven and hell as they concern Christian ethics, human subjectivity, that is, how we understand our personhood, personal identity after death, and such like. In the twentieth century, the great Protestant theological minds (Rudolf Bultmann, Karl Barth, Jürgen Moltmann, Eberhard Jüngel and Wolfhart Pannenberg) did not have these matters as their central concern. They talked variously about hope, eschatology, and the coming of God's kingdom on earth, but tended to downplay the doctrine of heaven and especially its personal aspects.

Karl Barth writes about creation reaching its goal and end once the created order has passed away. Human history, he says, will one day be over and its possibilities exploited: 'The time will come when the created world as a whole will only have been … It will not need any continuance of temporal existence.'[2] Yet he says relatively little about heaven and hell. One of his objectives was to reject Neoplatonic philosophical conceptions of the immortality of the soul as distinct from eternal life, and this was a key focus of his concerns. Barth's strong contrast between time as we know it and eternity in God tends to dissolve any sense of time in eternity.

Human history, says Barth, will not need to progress further, it will have fulfilled its purpose. Historical life as we know it will be over: its development will be completed, he writes, 'its notes sounded, its colours revealed, its thinking thought, its words said, its deeds done.'[3] Time as we know it is swallowed up in eternity. In other words, Barth's work leaves behind problematic notions of eternity as merely perpetuity, for example, stretching out for an unlimited or indefinitely long period of time – endlessness. His vision of heaven is cast in terms of the termination and completion of human history, and pays relatively little attention to witness in Christian tradition to the inclusion and transformation of time in eternity. Sustained consideration of the hope of heaven for the person – such that neither time nor personal identity is lost and what it means to die in Christ is further explored – is missing.[4]

In some similarity, Jürgen Moltmann writes much about the kingdom of God coming on earth, historical eschatology (new heaven, new earth). His focus is on the Spirit of God's active presence in the world with a view to fostering humanity's respect for the created earth through adoration of the triune God.[5] So, for instance, in his book *God in Creation*, the chapter entitled 'Heaven and Earth' includes a subsection entitled 'the heaven of nature'. Moltmann's interests are with the glory of God's heaven as it will envelop the earth when creation is renewed. In his eschatology, he looks for the completion, blessing and sanctification of creation when God's will is finally done on earth.

In other words, Moltmann's focus is the renewal of the whole earth when it finally becomes God's footstool and is incorporated into the glory of heaven. After death, the individual person's history will not cease but will be transformed and somehow included in eternal life. Moltmann mentions this topic briefly. His guiding interest, however, is not personal eschatology but the future of all creation in God. His work serves the Church well at a time of environmental crisis when believers need theological guidelines for a doctrine of ecology. My point, however, is that neither Barth nor Moltmann pays as much attention as they might have done to the hope of heaven. The emphasis in both is on God's eternal existence and God's relation to all creation.

Does this relative lack of attention to the more personal aspects of the hope of heaven matter? Yes! It matters intensely – because it undermines the unity of the material and spiritual aspects of Christian believers' thinking about work. It also undermines believers' ability to think about the continuity in their lives, before and after death, of the significance of work undertaken.

Heaven in Orthodox iconography

Orthodox iconography has much to teach on these matters. Icons do not typically transgress beyond the boundaries of biblical teaching. Hence there are no icons of heaven. Innumerable icons of the saints are portrayed, however, as transfigured and transformed in Christ. The saints are not painted as historical likenesses (to convey what these people looked like during their lives) but in ways that represent the theological truth of the existence of the saints in heaven, 'changed from glory into glory', to cite the final verse of Charles Wesley's hymn 'Love divine, all loves excelling'.

Icons are shunned sometimes by Western Christians for fear of giving undue reverence to an object, or that such images will distract the believer from worship of the one true God. Nothing could be farther from the experience of devout Orthodox believers, who ground their veneration of icons in a theology of the incarnation – the invisible became visible; the infinite took finite form. The icon stirs in the faithful a desire to see beyond the visible and finite and to gaze with the heart upon our Redeemer, whose Spirit surrounds each person and congregation as they pray.

Icons of the saints arouse more unease, typically, than icons of scenes from Holy Scripture. Even those Western Christians who find it spiritually edifying to pray with icons of the crucifixion, resurrection, ascension, the annunciation and Mother of Christ cradling her child, often find themselves uncomfortable before icons of the saints. I confess to having experienced this reticence and unease myself.

The suggestion in this section is that icons of the saints are representations of biblical teaching that witness to the deification of those in heaven who have appeared before the throne of God and are drawn ever closer into communion with him. Consider the icon of St Nicholas on p. 98. It speaks to viewers of the hope of heaven, and the interpenetration in Christian living of the material and spiritual, earthly and heavenly, human and divine.

Few details in the icon represent Nicholas's earthly life. Orthodox believers would be familiar nonetheless with basic information about this. He was renowned for his defence of orthodoxy at the First Ecumenical Council of Nicaea (AD 325), founding hospitals and hostelries for the poor, and using his wealth for the relief of families, widows and children. The icon does not, however, stimulate the imagination to recall the events of his life. Icons might allude to instances in a saint's life – their importance is not lost. Yet there is no encouragement to the imagination to fill in historical details.

The icon painters were concerned minimally to represent the saint as he actually looked during their lifetime; this is not

portraiture. The spiritual truth of their transformed existence in heaven, where their vision of God is complete, is much more important than visual accuracy or verisimilitude. Nor do icons of the saints invite viewers to conjure up images of what heaven might be like. There is no need to imagine what heaven is like beyond biblical witness to 'the inheritance of the saints in light' (Colossians 1:12). Yet to pray with this icon is to be drawn into the experience of Nicholas and all the saints in the presence of God, and to know something of their transfiguration.

Transfiguration

The icon teaches that there is a bodily resurrection and a continuation (albeit transfigured) of the saint's earthly identity. Even the smallest and most insignificant detail of the saint's transfigured identity represents something of the existence of the saints in heaven. His entire life – including, we may suppose, all that was worthy in his theological labours, work with hospitals and hostelries and so on – is transfigured against a backdrop of gold, which represents the faith that they are in heaven with Christ until he comes again in his glory to establish heaven throughout the galaxies.

The mandorla (halo of light) indicates that the truths represented by the icons are not available to historical investigation but only to faith. This message of faith is one of potentially astonishing inspiration, however. Like most icons of the saints, the icon of St Nicholas portrays him with an earth-coloured face. This recalls the Hebrew play on the words *Adam* and *adamah* (earth). He was a human being like the rest of us. Yet the sensory organs are large. His eyes gaze at the Lord (Luke 2:30). His ears are enlarged to hear the Word of God. His mouth is closed because true contemplation demands silence and the spiritual body needs no earthly nourishment. The wrinkled forehead implies wisdom.

The dominant feature of the icon is its golden radiance. Gold signifies the glory of God in heaven as it is now shared by the saints. This human existence, complete with all its meagre offerings to God, shares the very life divine. What story, then, does the icon tell of the significance of Nicholas's work on earth and its relation to what happens in heaven? What, then, has happened in the icon to the earthly work completed by Nicholas? It is transfigured.

THE HOPE OF HEAVEN GIVES ETERNAL SIGNIFICANCE TO EARTHLY WORK

Protestant scholar Darrell Cosden develops this idea of the unity in Christ of the earthly and heavenly, material and spiritual, in his book *The Heavenly Good of Earthly Work*. He argues directly from the resurrection rather than indirectly via icons of the saints. Yet his conclusion is similar: *the resurrection means that the work we do has eternal significance.*

Like icons of the saints, the central message is that of hope and transfiguration. Cosden's claim with respect to New Testament teaching that all that is included in Christ's incarnation and resurrection will become holy in God's sight: 'For in him all the fullness of God was pleased to dwell, and through him God was pleased to reconcile to himself all things, whether on earth or in heaven, by making peace through the blood of his cross' (Colossians 1:19–20). Christ's redemptive work involves bringing everything under his lordship: the resurrection 'has as much to do with transforming mundane and even hostile earthly realities as it does the religious aspects of life'.[6] *Even the daily grind at the office has significance beyond this life because of its inclusion in God's future. Nothing included in Christ's resurrection will be lost.*

The point here is not that the work we do helps us to achieve immortality. The gospel is not based on good works but on faith. Salvation is not by what we do (Galatians 2:16) but through faith which is the gift of God: 'For by grace you have been saved through faith, and this is not your own doing; it is the gift of God' (Ephesians 2:8–10). So-called 'works righteousness' is not a part of biblical Christian witness. Rather, Cosden's concern is that the strength of Protestant reaction against 'works righteousness' can tip into an improper disregard for the eternal significance of the work we do. To suppose that everyday work bears no eternal significance is just as irresponsible theologically, says Cosden, as 'works righteousness'.

What's the heavenly good of earthly work? asks Darrel Cosden. Lots! 'For truly I tell you,' says Jesus, 'whoever gives you a cup of water to drink because you bear the name of Christ will by no means lose the reward' (Mark 9:41). Giving a cup of water to the thirsty person is somehow incorporated into the kingdom of God; no act is futile because Christ has risen. If true, the implication is that everything that we do in the workplace matters because it has eternal significance. It matters unto eternity whether, for example, we teach our classes to the best of our ability, respect our clients, offer employees living wages, maintain a safe working environment, or do the accounts honestly.

Whilst there is a sense in which this earth will pass away (Matthew 5:17–18, 24:35), the resurrection means that nothing true, good or beautiful about our work will be lost to the Lord but included mysteriously in the mystery of the ages: 'when you were buried with him in baptism, you were also raised with him through faith in the power of God, who raised him from the dead' (Colossians 2:12). This is the Christian hope. Here is the reason to consecrate all our work to God in Christ's name. Its significance within divine providence will be preserved to eternity.

'AS IN HEAVEN, SO ON EARTH'

How, then, may guidance for an ethic of work be derived from Jesus' words: 'as in heaven, so on earth'? Is heaven a place of work? If so, in what sense? Can we really learn to work on earth 'as in heaven'? Do we know enough about work in heaven for this to be possible?

At the heart of this section are Jesus' words in the prayer that he gave his disciples:

> Our Father in heaven,
> hallowed be your name.
> Your kingdom come.
> Your will be done,
> on earth as it is in heaven. (Matthew 6:9–10)

Jesus' prayer is that our earthly living in obedience to God's will be conducted as in heaven, that is, as perfectly as God's will is done in heaven. The work of heaven is the doing of God's will – which is fulfilled in love (Matthew 22:37; Romans 13:10; Galatians 5:14).

This familiar English translation, rendering the imperatives of the Greek text, carries the implication that persons are active: they have the capacity to think about God's will, to choose to do God's will, and to enjoy living in communion with the Spirit of God; heaven cannot be inactive and without work because God's will is done. 'As in heaven so on earth' (*hōs en ouranō kai epi tēs gēs*): the coming of God's kingdom and the doing of God's will shall indeed happen or come to pass, by means of more than human effort.

There seems to be tension between 'the hallowing of God's name and doing of his will' as *work to be done* and as something that will happen regardless of whether we pray for and desire it. It is tempting when faced with such a tension to pose it in either/or terms. But this is surely a temptation to be resisted. Good and fruitful human relationships are rarely either active or passive but both intermingled in a dynamic of love. (Compare Philippians 2:13–14.)

Augustine expresses something of the paradox of activity and passivity as the Spirit of God works in and with believers. He sets this same paradox in motion within the dynamic of love when he writes:

> Following after God is the desire of happiness; to reach God is happiness itself ... He is light itself; we get enlightenment from Him. The greatest commandment, therefore, which leads to happy life, and the first, is this: 'Thou shalt love the Lord thy God with all thy heart, and soul, and mind.' For to those who love the Lord all things issue in good.[7]

Love for God, like the truest erotic passion, is a response to love already shown. Here the active and passive components of love mingle beautifully. To desire the Lord God with all one's heart, soul and mind, and seek to follow after him, is to know the intermingling of the active and passive aspects of work within the dynamic of love.

Gianlorenzo Bernini's statue *The Ecstasy of St Teresa of Avila* offers an answer that I believe to be compatible with Jesus' words and Augustine's teaching in this respect. It depicts a remarkable mystic experience related by St Teresa, in *The Life of Saint Teresa of Avila by Herself* (ch. 29), in which an angel appears to her in bodily form and pierces her heart with his spear. Her bliss of spiritual love is known in physical ecstasy; her great love of God appears to be extremely hard work and somewhat exhausting. Desire is aroused by knowledge and experience of the object of love; 'work is love, and love is work'. This is the work of heaven!

WORK AND THE HOPE OF HEAVEN'S REST

So far, I have argued that heaven is not a place of indolence, inertia, sluggishness or quiescence because God's name is honoured (Matthew 6:9–10). The fulfilment of God's will requires the active engagement of personal beings, activity and the expenditure of energy toward an end – namely, the glorifying of God. Other New Testament passages also suggest that the saints in heaven do more than relax on puffy clouds:

- Philippians 2:10 implies that those in heaven bow the knee at the name of Jesus;
- Philippians 3:20 speaks of 'citizenship in heaven' which suggests that inhabitants have privileges and duties;
- Hebrews 11:16 implies a better place or city (Greek *polis*) prepared by God for those who became heirs to righteousness in Christ.
- Revelation 5:3 describes a throne room in which no one in heaven or on earth was worthy to loose the seals of the scroll and open it: 'But one of the elders said to me, "Do not weep ..." '

Again, I must emphasise that a proper agnosticism is in order. We cannot gaze into the vaults of heaven or observe the saints in glory fulfilling the law of love, and so remain ignorant of heaven's glories. Yet biblical witness suggests that heaven is a reality on which we may set our hearts and minds eagerly (Hebrews 11:16), and for which the faithful might properly yearn (2 Corinthians 5:2; Philippians 3:17–20; Colossians 1:5).

What, however, about the relationship between work and rest? How does the hope of heaven's rest, and its character, inform our thinking about earthly work? We know from the Scriptures that heaven is where God has prepared a place for us (John 14:1–11), an incorruptible and undefiled inheritance awaiting those saved by the power of God (1 Peter 1:4). John's Gospel records Jesus' promise of a dwelling place prepared for each person (John 14:2–3). This passage is read at many funeral services because its beautiful words suggest the boundless hospitality of our God who will welcome the faithful home. The famous words in the closing paragraph of Augustine's *City of God* are as follows:

> There we shall be at rest and see,
> We shall see and love,
> We shall love and praise. (22.30)

Heaven, for Augustine, is a place of rest, comfort and peace. Of interest in this section is the nature of this rest, how we get to glimpse it, and how hope of this rest bears upon our engagement with earthly work and workplaces. Three points will be made:

- Firstly, a glimpse of heaven's rest is found in the *freedom* that believers enjoy on Sundays *from the ultimacy of everyday work.*
- Secondly, more than relaxation or leisure, the character of heaven's rest is a deep, relational *arriving at peace* with God.
- Thirdly, the hope of heaven's rest teaches deep patterns of repair, restoration and renewal for workplaces today.

Freedom from the ultimacy of everyday work

Glimpses of heaven's rest might feel few and far between for most of us in this life. Yet the spiritual truth of every Sunday gets us close. Despite the awkwardness that many Christian people often feel these days about 'keeping Sunday special' by refraining from certain activities, Sunday/Sabbath-day renunciation of the ultimacy of work frees us from the kind of attachment to work that attributes it significance apart from God: 'by making man free from himself it [the Sabbath] makes himself free for himself ... [and] for God in a special way,' writes Karl Barth.[8] The Sabbath teaches *freedom from* the seeming ultimacy of earthly work and its related concerns, and *freedom for* both self and God.

One of my grandmothers was very strict about what children were allowed, and not allowed, to do on Sundays. As a teenager, I thought her restrictions to be a hangover from her own late Victorian and Edwardian upbringing. Recently, I am more inclined (in theory, if not in practice) to sympathise with the uncompromising tenor of her beliefs. 'If you don't make time for worship,' she once said, 'you are taking yourself too seriously.'

Father Thomas Hopko of St Vladimir's Orthodox Theological Seminary, New York, makes a similar point about resting with God during the week. Every weekday, says Fr Thomas, try to spend half an hour in prayer and Bible study every day, except those days when the pressures of work are exceptionally great. On those days when the pressure is greatest one should spend a whole hour![9] Both he and my grandmother make a point not only about resting in God but also about freedom: true freedom is found in God, not in the constraints and necessities of everyday work; they have no ultimacy.

Sabbath rest

From the earliest days of the Christian Church, celebration of the Lord's Day was a *thinking with* and *rethinking of* the meaning of the Sabbath. The earliest Christians did not dispense with the covenants that God made with his people Israel, however. In the early Church, Christian celebration of the Lord's Day did not ignore the Sabbath as a holy day of blessing and delight when 'all creatures of God bless him', but regarded the Lord's Day as the fulfilment of the saving covenants made with Israel.[10] 'For us, the true Sabbath', writes Gregory the Great, 'is the person of our Redeemer, our Lord Jesus Christ.'[11]

This means, for our purposes, that to grasp fully how the resurrection determines, shapes and directs a Christian theology and ethical understanding of work, we must reread biblical accounts of the Sabbath and learn afresh from Judaism how the Sabbath teaches us a biblical account of work.[12]

For Judaism, of course, the Sabbath is about much more than relaxation and refreshment – though it is about these. The Sabbath, writes Jewish scholar Abraham Heschel, is the reason for the week: without it, we'd have no 'window in eternity that opens into time'.[13] The Sabbath is the day that lends significance to the week because it teaches the holiness of time; it is the day in which the clattering of commerce is silenced and the soul learns to rejoice in God, the day in which Israel comes like a bride to meet with her groom and the world becomes a place of rest:

> the art of keeping the seventh day is the art of painting on the canvas of time the mysterious grandeur of the climax of creation: as He sanctified the seventh day, so shall we. The love of the Sabbath is the love of man for what he and God have in common.[14]

Sabbath time set aside for God is like the time in a marriage given to the most intimate communion. Even thinking about work allows its cares and troubles to crowd in upon the Sabbath's time of rest and joy. More than relaxation or leisure in order that we might return to work refreshed, the Sabbath signifies something about God's purposes for creation, and sets the priorities for how we live. Jewish scholar Peter Ochs puts it beautifully in a discussion of Psalm 105:

> Reference to the heavens turns the worshipper's (and the psalmist's) attention to all God's creatures, who are now addressed as fellow singers of praise: 'Let the ocean roar … the field rejoice … the trees of the forest.' All creatures share in the worshippers' activity of praising the Creator, and this implies that, regardless of whether they all 'speak' and regardless of whether we share in any collective action, all creatures share with me the capacity and obligation to sing praises to YHWH.[15]

Jews and Christians think differently about the Sabbath. Together, however, we affirm that the Sabbath/Sunday is a time of remaking of body, mind and soul, in sheer enjoyment of the presence of God.

This acknowledged, we must note that the early Church took to heeding the fourth commandment on the first day after the Sabbath. This was not a rebellion against Judaism but a fulfilment of its hopes. The day we now call Sunday was the day when Jesus rose (Mark 16:2, 9; Luke 24:1; John 20:1), when he appeared to the two disciples on the road to Emmaus (Luke 24:13–35), the eleven Apostles gathered together (Luke 24:36; John 20:19) and later to Thomas (John 20:26).[16] The day of Pentecost – fifty days following the Sabbath of the Passover (Leviticus 23:11) – also fell on a Sunday (Acts 2:1). For all these reasons, the earliest Christians met in liturgical assembly on the day after the Jewish Sabbath.

In other words, the meaning of Sabbath rest for the earliest Christians was found in Christ Jesus himself. The writer to the Hebrews explains this. For him/her, the promise of heaven's rest is a deep, relational *arriving at peace* with God through Christ's actions on our behalf. The hope of this peace can have a profound affect upon one's attitude to the worries of earthly work. More than relaxing in style, with a long, cool lemonade after a long day's work (though nothing wrong with that!), the hope of heaven's rest yields a fundamental assurance of salvation because of what Christ has done. He is mediator of the new covenant that brings liberation from sins through his intercession so that believers are free to enter the sanctuary with confidence (Colossians 1:22).

Believers may have confidence to enter the sanctuary by the blood of Jesus and because he pleads on our behalf (Hebrews 7:25, 10:19–22). 'Therefore, my friends,' says the author of the letter to the Hebrews,

> since we have confidence to enter the sanctuary by the blood of Jesus, by the new and living way that he opened for us through the curtain (that is, through his flesh), ... let us approach with a true heart in full assurance of faith, with our hearts sprinkled clean from an evil conscience and our bodies washed with pure water. (Hebrews 10:19–22).

More than relaxation or leisure in order that we might return to work refreshed, heaven's rest – anticipated in every Sunday's rest – is a deep, relational *arriving at peace* with God.

Repair

We probably all have our personal hopes and preferences about what heaven's rest will be like – cream cakes without calories, no bills to pay, meeting again with loved ones. With respect to our topic, however, insights from Judaism speak directly to our concerns.

An important word in some recent Jewish theology and ethics is 'repair'. Witness the pragmatic aspects of Steven Kepnes' liturgical and scriptural reasoning (see Chapter 3 above). Liturgical and scriptural reasoners are typically Jews, Christians and Muslims who meet, read and reason together for the healing of our separate communities and repair of the world. We come together, says Steven Kepnes, to read and reason with our scriptures: 'We then return to our religious and academic institutions with renewed energy to bring criticism and healing to our institutions.'[17]

The pragmatic aspects of liturgical and scriptural reasoning are expounded by the Jewish scholars Peter Ochs, Steven Kepnes and others in terms of a logic of repair, or corrective activity. These pragmatic ways of thinking (*tikkun olam*, to use the Jewish phrase for the moral labour of mending the world) arise in part from Jewish thinking about the Sabbath. As Kepnes writes of the liturgies of the Jewish Sabbath and Day of Atonement, 'the foreigner becomes fellow creature through the community of prayer ... love for the fellowman, God's love for humans and human love for God are established through the mediation of the festival of the Shabbat.'[18] The Sabbath is a time for the repair and healing of oneself, of human relationships, our relationship with the environment, and much more.

The deep patterns of repair, restoration and renewal found in Scripture and liturgical worship anticipate heaven's rest. They are also the reason also why the Church exists *for the whole world*.

This is not a matter of Christians taking the high moral ground in discussions with work colleagues or in executive reports. The gospel cannot be reduced to moral precepts that keep society on the right course. Learning patterns of repair, restoration and renewal from the Scriptures, worship and the hope of heaven, is *not* like the cartoon by Harley Schwardron that depicts a health-food shop with a sign in the window: 'New! For the corporate executive – "moral fibre" supplements'.[19] 'Do not judge, so that you may not be judged. For with the judgement you make you will be judged, and the measure you give will be the measure you get' (Matthew 7:1–2). Jesus warned expressly against such moralising. Rather, until called to our heavenly rest, our business is realising its patterns of repair, restoration and renewal.

Many models are available in the Bible to help us think from this future and discern practical judgements with reference to it.

- The 'Salt and Light' model focuses on the public presence of the Church and also the explicit presence of disciples of Christ in workplaces. So, for instance, business people appear on the BBC *Songs of Praise* TV programme and speak openly about how they engage with competitors, market their products, and deal with customers. Executives and entrepreneurs might attend a monthly prayer breakfast at which their presence affirms publicly that the gospel places requirements on how they conduct their affairs. A worker might choose to wear a crucifix or cross to signify discipleship. A teenager might start a Christian Union (CU) at college. Someone recently moved into sheltered housing might book the common room for hymn singing. A vicar might co-ordinate a weekly column on 'workplace ethics' in the local newspaper.
- The 'Yeast in the Dough' model gives expression to the more hidden witness of believers who might not have 'come out' as Christians in the workplace but approach their employment as the outworking of deeply held convictions with respect to social justice, the quality of care that should be enjoyed by those in need, the importance of job creation, and much more. For instance, a personnel manager might be especially careful to use hotel chains that employ unionised rather than non-unionised staff because this impacts significantly upon working conditions in those hotels. A school governor might press for additional energy-saving measures in the plans for the new school to reduce carbon dioxide in the atmosphere. A housewife or

house-husband might, for the same reason, try to prepare meals that use less meat. A hairdresser might keep a copy of *The Tablet* or other church newspaper in the magazine rack.

- The 'Wisdom' model might be adopted by leaders in public life who deem that, in some instances, mention of 'God' might add nothing to the discussion. A committed believer can speak in the public square of 'the wisdom of God' without explicit reference to 'the will of God', i.e., the former can be spoken of apart from the subject of whom it is predicated. As the Jewish theologian David Novak writes: 'If God has willed something because it is wise, and if that wisdom is accessible to any rational person, then what difference does it make *who* has willed it? Is it not something that is *always to be willed by anyone*?[20] Theologically, this 'Wisdom' model presupposes an understanding of natural law – understood here as 'any concept of ethical thinking which grounds morality in some kind of objective fashion to which human behaviour in general and positive law in particular ought to conform and which is known by man through his natural faculties as distinguished from knowledge obtained through Divine Revelation'.[21]

These, and many other models for thinking about patterns of repair, restoration and renewal found in Holy Scripture and Christian tradition, presuppose that the gospel of Christ is for everyone. The consequence of the primordial fall is that we have been banished from paradise; all people who come from the seed of Adam are participants in ancestral sin and our work is subject to corruption, disease, toil and death. The hope of the resurrection is that all creation will once again be filled with the healing love of God.

Until that day, nothing in all creation, including the darkest and most cruel of workplaces, is devoid of the presence of God. The Word who became flesh, and whose flesh we eat, is the Word through whom all things came into being. The holy sacrament that we celebrate amidst the company of the faithful points to a sacramentality of all creation that has not yet been revealed or realised. In other words, the eucharistic celebration instills in Christ's disciples an attitude of mind that sees all creation as destined for glory. Until that day, and because of its coming, participants in Christ's resurrection have both the reason and the strength to struggle for decent, humane work.

NOTES

Chapter 1: THANK GOD IT'S FRIDAY?

1. Mark Twain, 'The Lost Napoleon' in *Mark Twain: A Biography* Vol. II, Part 2. Available at <http://mark-twain.classic-literature.co.uk/mark-twain-a-biography-volume-ii-part-2-1886-1900/ebook-page-37.asp> (accessed 17/01/07).
2. Mark Twain, *The Adventures of Tom Sawyer*, available at <http://mark-twain.classic-literature.co.uk/the-adventures-of-tom-sawyer/ebook-page-06.asp> (accessed 17/01/07).
3. Oscar Wilde, 'The Remarkable Rocket' in *The Happy Prince and Other Tales* (1888). Available at <http://www.online-literature.com/wilde/179/> (accessed 11/07/09).
4. Adam Scott, <http://www.dilbert.com/> (accessed 11/07/09).
5. Donald E. Simanek, 'A Glossary of Frequently Misused or Misunderstood Physics Terms and Concepts', available at <http://www.lhup.edu/~dsimanek/glossary.htm> (accessed 16/08/06).
6. André Gorz, *Reclaiming Work: Beyond the Wage-Based Society* (Cambridge: Polity Press, 1999; reprinted 2005), p. 3.
7. Gorz, *Reclaiming Work*, p. 3. Emphasis original.
8. Gorz, *Reclaiming Work*, p. 1.
9. Recounted by Gilbert Meilander (ed.) in *Working: Its Meaning and Its Limits* (Notre Dame, IN: University of Notre Dame Press, 2003), p. 1.
10. J. P. Toner, *Leisure and Ancient Rome* (Cambridge: Polity Press, 1995), p. 19.
11. Toner, *Leisure and Ancient Rome*, p. 15.
12. Miroslav Volf, *Work in the Spirit: Toward a Theology of Work* (Eugene, OR: Wipf and Stock Publishers, 2001), p. 102.
13. John Calvin, *Institutes of the Christian Religion*, ed. John T. McNeill and Ford Lewis Battle, Vol. 20 of the Library of Christian Classics (Philadelphia: Westminster Press, 1960), pp. 724–5.
14. For an account of the industrial 'work ethic', see Zygmunt Bauman, *Work, Consumerism and the New Poor* (Buckingham: Open University Press, 1998), Ch. 1, *passim*.
15. George Herbert, 'The Elixir' in John N. Wall, Jr (ed.), *George Herbert: The Country Parson, The Temple* (New York: Paulist Press, 1981), p. 311.
16. Volf, *Work in the Spirit*, p. x.

17. I use the summary offered by Simon Deakin and Gillian S. Morris, *Labour Law*, 4th edn (Oxford and Portland, OR: Hart Publishing, 2005), p. 1.
18. Timothy Jenkins, 'An ethical account of ritual: an anthropological description of the Anglican Daily Offices', *Studies in Christian Ethics* 15.1 (2002), pp. 1–10, esp. p. 1.
19. David Peterson, *Engaging with God* (Nashville, TN: Abingdon Press, 1992), pp. 17–19.
20. Mark Greene, *Supporting Christians at Work* (*without Going Insane*) (London: The London Institute for Contemporary Christianity, 2001), p. 5.
21. M. G. Kline, *Kingdom Prologue* (Eugene, OR: Wipf and Stock, 1993), p. 54.
22. Karl Barth, *Church Dogmatics* III/4 (Edinburgh: T&T Clark, 1961), p. 518.

Chapter 2: EASTER SATURDAY AND THE CURSE OF WORK TODAY

1. Hesketh Pearson, *The Life of Oscar Wilde* (London: Methuen, 1954), p. 202.
2. Karl Barth, *Church Dogmatics* IV/2 (Edinburgh: T&T Clark, 1958), p. 497.
3. John Milton, *Paradise Lost*, Book 9 (1667–69 edn). Published by Project Gütenberg and available at <http://www.literature.org/authors/milton-john/paradise-lost/chapter-09.html> (accessed 11/07/09).
4. As reported by Mark Oliver and agencies, 'Archbishop Urges Church to Consider Slavery Reparations', Guardian Unlimited, Monday 26 March 2007, at <http://www.guardian.co.uk/religion/Story/0,,2043058,00.html> (accessed 29/03/2007).
5. See Jeanne Segil, 'Slavery Continues Today', Tuesday 20 March 2007, at <http://memorytoaction.blogspot.com/2007/03/slavery-continues-still-today.html> (accessed 29/03/2007).
6. See <http://www.humantrafficking.org/> (accessed 11/07/09).
7. Established by Treaty of Versailles (1919) to abolish injustice, hardship and deprivation, the International Labor Organisation (ILO) has since then addressed the problem of labour conditions involving 'injustice, hardship and privation'. Recognising the need for flexibility in order to take account of variations in national circumstances, conditions and practices, it promotes fundamental principles and rights at work. International labour standards are, it claims, *universal* in character. The ILO Convention, among other provisions, protects workers' freedom of association and right to organise, prohibits the use of forced or compulsory labour, prohibits discrimination against women in the workplace, takes a stand against child labour. Signing a United Nations or ILO Convention indicates that a nation state intends to be bound by its provisions, even though there are mechanisms for indicating provisions by which a state does not wish to be bound, and for laying out particular interpretations. Its work, claim its supporters, has changed attitudes and practices towards vulnerable people in most, if not all, countries of the world.
8. See Third World Network at <http://www.twnside.org.sg> (accessed 27/07/03).
9. See TUC Online, World Day for Decent Work (WDDW) at <http://www.tuc.org.uk/theme/index.cfm?theme=wddw> (accessed 7/10/08).

10. TUC Online, World Day for Decent Work.
11. *Willing Slaves: How the Overwork Culture Is Ruling Our Lives* is the title of Madeleine Bunting's study of overwork and despair in British workplaces today (London: Harper Perennial, 2005). She analyses the impact on individuals and families of employers 'wanting blood' (p. xiv) to the extent that home life is damaged, workplaces have rising incidences of depression, company loyalty counts for little, and the threat of redundancy is commonplace.
12. Changing Times – The TUC's fortnightly online bulletin on work–life balance issues. Available at <http://www.tuc.org.uk/work_life/tuc-12801-f0.cfm> (accessed 11/07/09).
13. The Work Foundation, 'Public Sector Work–Life Balance is more Rhetoric than Reality', 7 December 2006. Available at <http://www.theworkfoundation.com/aboutus/media/pressreleases/publicsector worklifebalanceismorerhetoricthanreality.aspx> (accessed 05/10/07).
14. Equal Opportunities Commission, 'Policy Statement: Facts about Dads Today', available at <http://83.137.212.42/sitearchive/eoc/Defaulta386.html ?page=15444> (accessed 11/07/09), citing M. O'Brien and I. Shemilt, *Working Fathers: Earning and Caring* (Manchester: Equal Opportunities Commission, 2003).
15. National Statistics, *Less Time for Voluntary Work: Economic Trends January 2004* (London: ONS, 2004), p. 1.
16. The Samaritans, *Stressed Out Survey 2007*. Details at <http://www.samaritans.org/your_emotional_health/managing_stress/managing_workplace_stress.aspx> (accessed 11/07/09).
17. Mental Health Foundation, *Burning Out or Burning Bright?* (2001), available at <http://www.mentalhealth.org.uk/publications/?EntryId5=38564> (accessed 9/11/09).
18. Anonymous article available at <http://www.geocities.com/CapitolHill/Lobby/3609/lib_whyfreegan.html> (accessed 11/12/05).
19. This information is derived from Freegan.info at <http://freegan.info/> (accessed 11/12/05).
20. Abraham Joshua Heschel, *Moral Grandeur and Spiritual Audacity: Essays Edited by Susannah Heschel* (New York: Farrar, Straus and Giroux, 1996), p. 75.
21. Oliver O'Donovan, *The Ways of Judgment* (Grand Rapids, MI: Eerdmans Publishing, 2005), p. 15.
22. O'Donovan, *The Ways of Judgment*, p. 20.
23. Fran, *Cartoon Stock* Catalogue Re. for0311 available at <http://www.cartoonstock.com/cartoonview.asp?search=site&catref=for0311&MA> (accessed 11/07/09).
24. O'Donovan, *The Ways of Judgment*, p. 88.
25. O'Donovan, *The Ways of Judgment*, p. 58.
26. Michel Quenot, *The Resurrection and the Icon*, trans. Michael Breck (Crestwood, NY: St Vladimir's Seminary Press, 1997), p. 82.
27. On this, see US Catholic Bishops, *Economic Justice for All: Pastoral Letter on Catholic Social Teaching and the U.S. Economy* (1986) available at <http://www.osjspm.org/economic_justice_for_all.aspx> (accessed 11/07/09).

28. Papal concern with workplace injustice was arguably undermined by the simultaneous attempt to discredit socialism. On this, see Jon D. Wisman, 'Christianity, John Paul II and the Future of Work', *International Journal of Social Sciences* Vol. 25 (1998), Issue 11, pp. 1658–71, esp. p. 1661.
29. Wisman, 'Christianity, John Paul II and the Future of Work', p. 1665.
30. Maryann O. Keating and Barry P. Keating, 'Economics as a Discipline: The Crossroads between John Paul II's Social Vision and Conservative Economic Thought', *International Journal of Social Sciences* Vol. 25 (1998), Issue 11/12, p. 1791, citing Lay Commission on Catholic Social Teaching and the US Economy, *Liberty and Justice for All* (Notre Dame, IN: The Brownson Institute, 1986).
31. On this, see Keating and Keating, 'Economics as a Discipline', p. 1801.
32. This phrase is used because the Lord wished to identify himself with the poor (Matt. 25:31–46) and took special care of them (cf. Ps. 12[11]:6; Luke 1:52f.).
33. See Keating and Keating, 'Economics as a Discipline', p. 1796.
34. Charles E. Curran, 'Catholic Social and Sexual Teaching: A Methodological Comparison' at <http://theologytoday.ptsem.edu/jan1988/v44–4-article1.htm> (accessed 11/07/09).

Chapter 3: RESURRECTION AND LITURGICAL MORAL REASONING

1. Walt Whitman, 'A Song for Occupations!' available at <http://www.daypoems.net/poems/1965.html> (accessed 11/07/09).
2. Dom Gregory Dix, *The Shape of the Liturgy* (London: Adam and Charles Black, 1945), p. 103.
3. Steven Kepnes, *Jewish Liturgical Reasoning* (Oxford: Oxford University Press, 2007), p. 10.
4. Kepnes, *Jewish Liturgical Reasoning*, p. 11.
5. See Peter Ochs, 'Through the Language of Hypothesis Formation', which is part of his *The Rules of Scriptural Reasoning* available at <http://etext.virginia.edu/journals/ssr/issues/volume2/number1/ssr02–01-e01.html> (accessed 11/07/09).
6. Ochs, 'Through the Language of Hypothesis Formation'.
7. Peter Ochs, 'Theosemiotics and Pragmatics', *The Journal of Religion* Vol. 72, No. 1 (January 1992), pp. 59–81, esp. p. 65.
8. Athanasius, *Against the Heathen*, Vol. IV in *Nicene and Post-Nicene Fathers, Second Series*, ed. Philip Schaff and Henry Wace, I, §1.
9. John Webster, *Holy Scripture* (Cambridge: Cambridge University Press, 2003), p. 23.
10. See Peter Ochs, 'Through the Language of Hypothesis Formation'.
11. Peter Ochs, *Peirce, Pragmatism and the Logic of Scripture* (Cambridge: Cambridge University Press, 2004), p. 115; Charles Hartshorne et al. (eds), *Collected Papers of C. S. Peirce* (Cambridge, MA: Harvard University Press, 1935–38), Vol. 5, para. 171.
12. *Babel* (2006), directed Alejandro Gonzales Inarritu in collaboration with the writer Guillermo Arriaga. For more information, see *The Internet Movie Database* at <http://www.imdb.com/title/tt0449467/> (accessed 11/07/09).

13. *The Divine Liturgy of St. John Chrysostom* available at <http://www.ocf.org/OrthodoxPage/liturgy/liturgy.html> (accessed 11/07/09).
14. Dix, *The Shape of the Liturgy*, p. 114.
15. Kepnes, *Jewish Liturgical Reasoning*, p. 60.
16. *The Divine Liturgy of St. John Chrysostom*.
17. Karl Barth, *Church Dogmatics* IV/3 First Half (Edinburgh: T&T Clark, 1961), p. 327.
18. Aaron Bacall, *Cartoon Stock*, Catalog Reference aba0123 available at <http://www.cartoonstock.com/cartoonview.asp?search=site&catref=aba0123&MA_Category=&ANDkeyword=ethics+taste&ORkeyword=&TITLEkeyword=&NEGATIVEkeyword> (accessed 11/07/09).
19. John Chrysostom's homily on Hebrews 9 is a classic exposition of the daily yet 'once for all' remembrance of Christ's death: 'What then? do not we offer every day? We offer indeed, but making a remembrance of His death, and this [remembrance] is one and not many. How is it one, and not many? Inasmuch as that [Sacrifice] was once for all offered, [and] carried into the Holy of Holies ... For we always offer the same, not one sheep now and tomorrow another, but always the same thing: so that the sacrifice is one. And yet by this reasoning, since the offering is made in many places, are there many Christs? but Christ is one everywhere, being complete here and complete there also, one Body. As then while offered in many places, He is one body and not many bodies.' Trans. Frederic Gardiner in *Nicene and Post-Nicene Fathers, First Series*, Vol. 14, ed. Philip Schaff (Buffalo, NY: Christian Literature Publishing Co., 1889); revised and edited for New Advent by Kevin Knight. See <http://www.newadvent.org/fathers/240217.htm>. This text is cited by Dix, *The Shape of the Liturgy*, p. 243.
20. Michael Pomazansky, *Orthodox Dogmatic Theology*, trans. Seraphim Rose (Platina, CA: St Herman Press, 2006), p. 287.
21. Dom Gregory Dix uses the phrase 'perpetually creative' with respect to the fruits of Christ's passion in the Church in *The Shape of the Liturgy*, p. 248.
22. *The Divine Liturgy of St. John Chrysostom*.
23. Adapted from Kenneth Fernandes, 'Prayer for the Workplace' available at: <http://wewo.blogspot.com/2006/04/prayer-for-work-place.html> (accessed 11/07/09).
24. Anglo-Catholic Socialism, *Prayers for Justice and Peace* available at <http://www.anglocatholicsocialism.org/prayers.html> (accessed 11/07/09).
25. Circle of Prayer, available at <http://www.circleofprayer.com/morning.html> (accessed 11/07/09).

Chapter 4: HUMAN RIGHTS IN THE WORKPLACE

1. Michèle Le Doeuff, *Hipparchia's Choice: An Essay Concerning Women, Philosophy, etc.*, trans. Trista Selous (New York: Columbia University Press, 1991; first published 1989), p. 28.
2. Le Doeuff, *Hipparchia's Choice*, pp. 29, 283.

3. Le Doeuff, *Hipparchia's Choice*, pp. 28, 255, 317.
4. John Chrysostom, *S. Chrysostom's Homilies on the Gospel of St Matthew* (Oxford: John Henry Parker, 1843), Homily XVI, sect. 10, p. 240; Augustine, *The City of God*, trans. Marcus Dods (New York: Random House, 1978), Bk IX, ch. 5, p. 285.
5. Thomas Aquinas, *Summa Theologia* (*ST*), trans. the Fathers of the English Dominican Province (New York: Benziger Bros. edition, 1947), III, *q.* 15, *a.* 9; online edition copyright © 2006 by Kevin Knight, available at <www.newadvent.org/summa>. This edition is cited in preference to *Summa Theologiae: Volume 19 – The Emotions* (I-II *q.* 22–30), ed. Eric D'Arcy (Cambridge: Cambridge University Press, 1967, reprinted 2006) because the latter translates *de passionibus animae* as the emotions rather than the passions or the passions of the soul.
6. Aquinas, *ST* III, *q.* 15, *a.* 9, *corpus.*
7. Elizabeth Uffenheimer-Lippens, 'Rationalized Passion and Passionate Rationality: Thomas Aquinas on the Relation between Reason and the Passions', *The Review of Metaphysics* 56 (March 2003), p. 544.
8. Aquinas, *ST* III, *q.* 15, *a.* 4, *corpus.*
9. Aquinas, *ST* III, *q.* 15, *a.* 4, *ad.* 1.
10. This observation is made by Uffenheimer-Lippens, 'Rationalized Passion and Passionate Rationality', p. 538.
11. Paul Gondreau, *The Passions of Christ's Soul in the Theology of St. Thomas Aquinas* (Münster: Aschendorff, 2002), p. 334.
12. Aquinas, *ST* III, *q.* 15, *a.* 1, *corpus.*
13. Aquinas, *ST* III, *q.* 41, *a.* 1, *corpus.*
14. P. J. O'Rourke, *On the Wealth of Nations* (New York: Atlantic Monthly Press, 2007), p. 40.
15. For more on this, see Esther D. Reed, *The Ethics of Human Rights* (Waco, TX: Baylor University Press, 2007), Ch. 3. I draw on Dietrich Bonhoeffer, *Ethics* in *The Dietrich Bonhoeffer Works* Vol. 6, trans. Reinhard Krauss et al. from the German edition ed. Ilse Tödt et al. (Minneapolis, MN: Fortress Press, 2005), pp. 186–7.
16. Paul Ricoeur makes a similar point in 'Love and Justice' in *Figuring the Sacred: Religion, Narrative and Imagination* (Minneapolis: Augsburg Fortress, 1995), p. 359.
17. E.g. Stanley Hauerwas, 'Abortion, Theologically Understood' in Paul T. Stallsworth (ed.), *The Church and Abortion: In Search of New Ground for Response* (Nashville: Abingdon Press, 1993), p. 50.
18. Available at <http://www.evangelicalsforhumanrights.org/> (accessed 23/02/09).
19. Vigen Guroian, *Rallying the Really Human Things* (Wilmington, DE: ISI Books, 2005), p. 214. *Hypostasis* is the Greek word adopted by the Council of Nicaea (AD 325) to designate personal existence.
20. O'Rourke, *On the Wealth of Nations*, p. 78.
21. O'Rourke, *On the Wealth of Nations*, p. 2.
22. O'Rourke, *On the Wealth of Nations*, p. 5.
23. O'Rourke, *On the Wealth of Nations*, p. 5.

24. O'Rourke, *On the Wealth of Nations*, p. 63.
25. Adam Smith, *The Theory of Moral Sentiments* (1759), Cambridge Texts in the History of Philosophy (Cambridge: Cambridge University Press, 2002), Part II, sect. ii, ch. I, para. 9. See also Adam Smith, *The Wealth of Nations* (1776; New York: Bantam Classics, 2003), Vol. II, Bk IV, Ch. 9.
26. O'Rourke, *On the Wealth of Nations*, p. 42.
27. P. J. O'Rourke cited at <http://www.brainyquote.com/quotes/authors/p/p_j_orourke.html> (accessed 26/11/08).
28. Vienna Declaration (second World Conference on Human Rights), para. 5. Noted by Henry J. Steiner and Philip Alston, *International Human Rights in Context: Law, Politics and Morals*, 2nd edn (Oxford: OUP, 2000), p. 237.
29. BBC News, 4 December 2008, 'DNA database "breach of rights" ' at <http://news.bbc.co.uk/1/hi/uk/7764069.stm> (accessed 01/01/09).
30. BBC News, 4 December 2009.
31. As reported by *Timesonline*, 5 December 2008: 'Police are ordered to destroy all DNA samples taken from innocent people' at <http://www.timesonline.co.uk/tol/news/politics/article5289312.ece> (accessed 01/01/09).
32. The European Trade Union Confederation, Legal Cases Laval Case (Vaxholm); information available at <http://www.etuc.org/r/847> (accessed 11/07/09).
33. The European Trade Union Confederation, Laval Case.
34. The European Trade Union Confederation, Legal Cases information available at <http://www.etuc.org/r/846> (accessed 01/01/09).
35. Lord Wedderburn, 'Collective Bargaining or Legal Enactment', *Industrial Law Journal* Vol. 29, No. 1 (March 2000), p. 13.
36. Wedderburn, 'Collective Bargaining or Legal Enactment', p. 15.
37. Catholic Bishops of England and Wales, *The Common Good* (Manchester: Gabriel Publications, 1996), § 92.
38. Catholic Bishops, *The Common Good*, § 93.
39. Thomas Aquinas, *Summa Contra Gentiles* (Notre Dame, IN, Notre Dame University Press, 1991), Bk 3a, ch. 69.
40. See O. J. Brown, *Natural Rectitude and Divine Law in Aquinas: An Approach to an Integral Interpretation of the Thomistic Doctrine of Law* (Toronto: Pontifical Institute of Medieval Studies, 1981), pp. 74–84.

Chapter 5: LOST VOCATIONS

1. I cite from Flamingo's publicity for its publication of *Cocaine Nights*.
2. J. G. Ballard, *Cocaine Nights* (London: Flamingo, 1996), p. 180.
3. Ballard, *Cocaine Nights*, p. 180.
4. Chris Hall, 'Interviews' in *Spike Magazine*, available at <http://www.spikemagazine.com/1100jgballard.php> (accessed 11/07/09).
5. J. G. Ballard, *Super-Cannes* (New York: Picador, 2002), p. 94.
6. Ballard, *Super-Cannes*, p. 38.
7. Ballard, *Super-Cannes*, p. 264.
8. Ballard, *Super-Cannes*, p. 259.

9. Chris Hall, 'Interviews'.
10. Stephen Moss, 'Mad about Ballard' at <http://books.guardian.co.uk/critics/reviews/0,5917,368007,00.html> (accessed 11/07/09).
11. Madeleine Bunting, *Willing Slaves: How the Overwork Culture Is Ruling Our Lives* (London: Harper Perennial, 2005).
12. Bunting, *Willing Slaves*, p. 100.
13. Bunting, *Willing Slaves*, p. 101.
14. See the Trades Union Congress (TUC) Work–Life Balance websites dedicated to giving employers guidance about how to help workers achieve a better work–life balance: <http://www.tuc.org.uk/work_life/> (accessed 11/07/09).
15. National Statistics, *Less Time for Voluntary Work: Economic Trends January 2004* (London: ONS, 2004), p. 1.
16. TUC Employment Research, 'Time to Stop Worker Abuse' (26 February 2007) at <http://www.tuc.org.uk/em_research/tuc-12990-f0.cfm> (accessed 11/07/09).
17. Anne E. Green and David Owen, *The Geography of Poor Skills and Access to Work* (York: The Joseph Rowntree Foundation, 2006), p. 9.
18. Green and Owen, *The Geography of Poor Skills*, p. 103.
19. David Hirsch et al., *Sustaining Working Lives and Practice* (York: The Joseph Rowntree Foundation, 2005), pp. 1–2.
20. John Paul II, General Audience, 30 November 1988: <http://www.vatican.va/holy_father/john_paul_ii/audiences/alpha/data/aud19881130en.html> (accessed 04/05/2009).
21. Thomas Hopko, *Theology of Work*, audio cassette available from St Vladimir's Seminary Press and Book Store (http://www.svspress.com), Track 3.
22. Marcel Sarot, 'Trinity and Church: Trinitarian Perspectives on the Identity of the Christian Community', unpublished paper for the Society for the Study of Theology (2009), p. 4.
23. The Lilly Endowment, Programs for the Theological Exploration of Vocation at <http://www.lillyendowment.org/religion_ptev.html> (accessed 11/07/09).
24. Christian Reflection, Centre for Christian Ethics, Baylor University, 'The Meaning of Vocation', at <http://www.baylor.edu/christianethics/Vocationstudyguide1.pdf> (accessed 11/07/09).
25. William A. Beardslee, *Human Achievement and Divine Vocation* (London: SCM Press, 1961), p. 17.
26. Terry Deal and Lee Bolman, *Leading with Soul: An Uncommon Journey of Spirit* (Hoboken, NJ: Wiley and Sons, 2001), p. 5.
27. I draw on Paul Ransome, *Work, Consumption and Culture: Affluence and Social Change in the Twenty-First Century* (London: Sage Publications, 2005), p. 16.
28. Beardslee, *Human Achievement and Divine Vocation*, p. 21.

Chapter 6: WILL THERE BE WORK IN HEAVEN?

1. Available at <http://ebiquity.umbc.edu/blogger/2005/11/13/Will-your-Blackberry-work-in-Heaven?/> (accessed 11/07/09).
2. Karl Barth, *Church Dogmatics* III/3 (Edinburgh: T&T Clark, 1961), pp. 87–8.
3. Barth, *CD* III/3, pp. 87–8.

4. I am indebted for many of these ideas to an unpublished paper by Church of Scotland minister Donald McEwan, entitled, 'Missing Persons: The Doctrine of Heaven in Twentieth Century Protestant Theology'.
5. This description is given at a website devoted to the Gifford Lectures from one series of which this particular book by Moltmann grew. Available at <http://www.giffordlectures.org/Browse.asp?PubID=TPGDIC&Volume=0&Issue=0&Summary=True> (accessed 11/07/09).
6. Darrell Cosden, *The Heavenly Good of Earthly Work* (Peabody, MA: Hendrickson Publishers, 2006), p. 65.
7. Augustine *On the Morals of the Manichaeans,* Ch. 11, trans. Richard Stothert, from *Nicene and Post-Nicene Fathers*, First Series, Vol. 4, ed. Philip Schaff (Buffalo, NY: Christian Literature Publishing Co., 1887.); rev. and ed. Kevin Knight for New Advent <http://www.newadvent.org/fathers/1402.htm>.
8. Karl Barth, *CD* III/4 (Edinburgh: T&T Clark, 1961), p. 60.
9. Thomas Hopko, *Theology of Work* (audio cassette available from St Vladimir's Seminary Press and Book Store: <http://www.svspress.com>), Track 3.
10. Abraham Joshua Heschel, *The Sabbath* (New York: Farrar, Straus and Giroux, 1975), p. 24, citing Sabbath morning liturgy.
11. Gregory the Great, *Verum autem sabbatum ipsum redemptorem nostrum Iesum Christum Dominum habemus, Epist.* 13, 1: *Corpus Christianorum Series Latina* 140A, 992. Cited in John Paul II, *Dies Domini* (1998). Available at <http://www.vatican.va/holy_father/john_paul_ii/apost_letters/documents/hf_jp-ii_apl_05071998_dies-domini_en.html> (accessed 11/03/2007).
12. 'The Sabbath commandment in its particularity explains all the other forms of the one divine commandment ... The concern of this particular day is indirectly that of all other days as well. This particular thing is the meaning of all the divine commands.' Barth, *CD* III/4, p. 55.
13. Heschel, *The Sabbath*, p. 16.
14. Heschel, *The Sabbath*, p. 16.
15. Peter Ochs in Randi Rashkover and C. C. Pecknold (eds), *Liturgy, Time and the Politics of Redemption* (Grand Rapids, MI: Eerdmans Publishing Co., 2006), p. 79.
16. John Paul II, Apostolic Letter *Dies Domini* (5 July 1998). Available at <http://www.vatican.va/holy_father/john_paul_ii/apost_letters/documents/hf_jp-ii_apl_05071998_dies-domini_en.html> (accessed 11/07/09).
17. See Steven Kepnes, 'A Handbook of Scriptural Reasoning' at <http://etext.lib.virginia.edu/journals/jsrforum/writings/KepHand.html> (accessed 26/11/08).
18. Steven Kepnes, *Jewish Liturgical Reasoning* (Oxford: OUP, 2007), pp. 58–9.
19. Harley Schwadron @ Cartoon Stock, Catalogue Ref: hsc0905. Available at <http://www.cartoonstock.com/cartoonview.asp?catref=hsc0905> (accessed 11/07/09).
20. David Novak, *Natural Law in Judaism* (Cambridge: Cambridge University Press, 1998), p. 18.

21. Stanley S. Harakas, 'The Natural Law Teaching in the Ante-Nicene Fathers and in Modern Greek Orthodox Theology', unpublished ThD thesis, Boston University School of Theology (1965), p. 4.

INDEX OF NAMES

INDEX OF SUBJECTS

INDEX OF SCRIPTURE REFERENCES